BEFORE YOU GET HERE

BAGGAGE TO DROP ON YOUR WAY TO HEAVEN

MICHAEL EVANS

© 2014 by Michael Evans
Published by Wholeness Ministries

Printed in the United States of America

All rights reserved. No part of this publication may be reproduced, stored in a retrieval system, or transmitted in any form or by any means- for example, electronic, mechanical, photocopy, recording-without the prior written permission of the publisher. The only exception is brief quotations in printed reviews.

ISBN - 978-0-9906679-4-0

Unless otherwise indicated all Scripture quotations are taken from the Holy Bible, New International Version, Copyright 1973, 1978, 1984, International Bible Society. Used by permission of Zondervan Bible Publishers.
Scripture marked NASB is taken from the New American Standard Bible. Copyright 1976, 1978, Moody Bible Institute. Used by permission of Moody Press.
Scripture marked NLT is taken from the New Living Translation. Copyright 1996, Tyndale Charitable Trust, Used by permission of Tyndale House Publishers, Inc.
Scripture marked The Message is taken from The Message, Copyright 1993, Eugene Peterson, Navpress Publishing Group.

DEDICATION

This book is dedicated to Francis MacNutt. Since our first meeting in the early nineties he believed in me and was a constant encouragement in the healing ministry. Francis became my spiritual father and mentor, helping me to understand that praying for healing should be a normal part of what we do. As a young enthusiastic minister I enjoyed praying for physical healing because I could see immediate results. Francis lovingly and patiently taught me that Inner Healing was also of great importance as it was often the key to physical healing. Through his loving and gentle modeling he helped me to see the value of spending time with people and helping them deal with the pain that often was so deep it immobilized them.

As I stood alongside him as we prayed for people in a variety of settings, I saw a man with the grace, gentleness and compassion of Jesus and said to myself, "That's what I want to be like."

I consider it an honor to have this man in my life as a friend.

ACKNOWLEDGEMENTS

When I first started praying for the sick in 1984 I was attracted to physical healing because I could see immediate results. At that point in my journey inner healing was something I didn't know much about but, from what I did know it was not appealing to me as it seemed to take a lot of time spent with one person. I am impatient by nature and this was an area of ministry I was glad to hand off to others. I wasn't far into praying for the sick when I came up against things that did not change when I prayed and saw that when we dealt with the roots of a person's pain then the physical healing would often be complete.

Soon God brought me to a place where I knew that I needed to write a book to help people identify the core of their pain and how to deal with it. Thus this book you hold in your hands.

Specifically in regards to this book:

My special thanks to my wife Jane who patiently read my early scribbling and lovingly suggested changes. To my daughter Jenny who took the first draft, slowly read through it and pointed out those areas that needed a rewrite to help them flow smoother and make more sense. To my editor Carla Kliever who read through the manuscript correcting my grammar and mistakes and suggesting what could be added to help clarify what I was trying to say. To Kim D'Angelo with Archer-Ellison Publishing who patiently handled the many details necessary to bring the book to the point where it could be published.

Lastly, to Amy Kliever a friend and the creative director of Blooming Footprint, http://amykliever.com, who designed the book cover which illustrates the heart of what I wrote.

CONTENTS

Preface	1
The Importance of Forgiveness	5
The Traps of Unforgiveness	9
A Look In The Mirror	25
I Will Never	39
Harmful Words, Harmful Connections	51
Let Yourself Be Loved By God	65
The Recovery Of Intimacy	79
God's Highest Purpose	89
What God Will Not Accept!	97
Unless You Change and Become as Little Children...	105
Conclusion	115
Notes	117
About Mike Evans	121
About Wholeness Ministries	123

PREFACE

I have been involved in the healing ministry since 1984. In the beginning my focus was on physical healing. This appealed to me because it was exciting to watch God heal and the results were usually apparent immediately. As I progressed in this journey it became obvious that there was, in many cases, a significant connection between physical healing and inner healing. Inner or deep-level healing is a ministry that specializes in freeing people from the emotional and spiritual "garbage" that we accumulate as we go through life.

Over the years people have encouraged me to write another book. The thought of writing another book was daunting and not a project I wished to tackle anytime soon. However, I was conducting a conference in Phoenix, Arizona, and had just finished telling a story about one of my associates at Wholeness Ministries who experienced the home-going of his beloved father – truly his best friend. Only days before his passing he called me from the hospital and asked me to pray for his father's healing over the phone. As he handed the phone to his father I began to pray and a name jumped into my head. So I asked his father, "Does this name mean anything to you? I'm trying to pray for your healing, but this is what I am hearing instead!" On the other end of the line my associate, his father and his mother were all stunned into shocked silence: the name I heard was the name of his mother's sister, his aunt, a person that his father had experienced great anger and bitterness towards many, many decades before! The father thought it was dealt with (forgotten more than forgiven, as we so often mistake!), but apparently it was not satisfactorily dealt with in God's eyes. In response to God supernaturally giving me the name of this person whom I had never heard of and knew nothing about, his father readily revisited his bitterness and forgave his sister-in-law more fully...a few days later he was taken home to Heaven.

Immediately after I finished telling this story, a gentleman I did not know stood up and said, "God said to tell you that you are too write another book and the title is *Before You Get Here!*"

It's not unusual when I am praying, to hear from God, as I shared in the story above. On rare occasions someone will come to me and say they have a message for me from God. When that happens I typically respond two ways. One, I consider the source, whether or not I feel they are credible. Second, I will wait for confirmation before I act on what they have said. In this case I knew that God for some time had been prompting me to write another book but I had been intentionally putting it off, as I wasn't sure what to write about. When I came home and shared this incident with my wife she immediately replied, "The subject is to be centered around inner healing and the sub-title is *Baggage To Drop On Your Way To Heaven*. For me, that was confirmation as I already felt that the gentleman who had spoken to me was credible. To then come home and have my wife so quickly affirm what he said was an affirmation that indeed God wanted me to write this book and the topic was to be inner deep-level healing, in this life, before Heaven.

As I prayed about this and began seriously thinking about what to write, God revealed to me that it is important to Him that we deal with all of our baggage before we die. That baggage is the stuff we carry around with us like unforgiveness, resentment, anger, bitterness, etc. Though I knew inner or deep-level healing was important, God made it clear to me that is a big deal to Him. In writing this book I believe that He has shown me a number of issues that He wants us to deal with before we get to heaven. Thus, the genesis of this book, *Before You Get Here.*

People come to our churches seeking healing for the numerous problems they face. They need healing spiritually, emotionally and physically. Often they are made to feel as if they shouldn't need healing once they have given their lives to Jesus. The Bible says that when you are born again you are a new creature in Christ. Christ's death on the cross took care of everything and "the old is gone, the new has come" (2 Corinthians 5:17). Therefore, some people believe we do not need to pay attention to the internal stuff that continues to keep us bound. If you simply look around the church at the people sitting next to you, it will quickly become apparent that we are not instantly transformed in our thinking and actions (2 Corinthians 3:18). People are still dealing with unforgiveness, anger, jealousy, drugs, pornography, bad marriages, broken families, etc. While our salvation is secured, it's obvious that our mind, will, emotions and body were not instantly perfected. We are meant to experience a continuing work of Christ in these areas.

The people who need help often make their way to secular counselors or to Christian counselors who use methods that do not always include using the power of prayer and guidance of the Holy Spirit. Without deliberately bringing the power of Jesus into the counseling relationship, they have only human power to solve superhuman problems. People can get help from those who practice secular counseling, but usually not complete healing.

Through the power of prayer we often see people freed up from the emotional and spiritual bondage that they have been living under for years.

May God bless you as you read this book and may He - through this tool and the power of His deep-level healing - open your mind to things you didn't realize were problems or other issues affecting your life. And may it also bring you into a place of freedom beyond what you thought was possible.

Mike Evans
Bakersfield, CA
June 9, 2014

Before You Get Here

THE IMPORTANCE OF FORGIVENESS

As I thought about Heaven, a couple of questions popped into my mind: "What's it going to be like and what will we do once we get there?" There have been numerous books written and personal experiences shared by those who have "died" and gone to heaven but then "returned." We have a difficult time believing some of these stories, but there are others from people whom we see as credible. And this makes it hard for us to discount what they are saying.

Beyond the experience of being "born again" at age twelve in a little church in Tulare, California, I didn't think much about what else I might have to deal with. That's because I was taught as a young man that once you have accepted Jesus into your life as your Lord and Savior you were guaranteed eternal life with God after you died. Your eternity would then be spent with God in Heaven. There was not a lot of thought given to dealing with issues from your past as all of that was forgiven and covered under the blood of Jesus.

I still believe that when you accept Christ you are saved. However, since then, I have learned that there is a continuing work of the Holy Spirit in our lives. The biblical teaching of Sanctification and Transformation involves attending to those things in our lives that keep us from growing into the fullness of Christ-likeness that God desires. These are things like anger, bitterness, jealousy, envy, lies, etc. What has become clear to me is that dealing with these issues is not just important for our emotional and spiritual health here on earth, but it is of vital importance to God. He wants us to resolve them before we get to heaven.

Unforgiveness issues are those things that most of us know about. We understand that we need to deal with them for our own emotional and physical health. But what about those issues that we have never heard about, such as inner vows or generational sins or soul ties? Many churches don't teach on these because they don't know about them or if they do know they are not sure how to approach them.

From the moment of our birth until our death, we accumulate baggage that is the result of things that people say and do to us, as well as things we say and do to others and ourselves. For much of my early walk with the Lord I had never heard of these types of issues and didn't have a clue that they existed and needed to be addressed. I certainly did not consider that before I died and went home to be with the Lord, He would not want me to bring this baggage with me. The abundant life he wanted for me was supposed to begin long before I went to Heaven, and it was not supposed to include baggage that robbed me of joy and fruitfulness.

THE BASICS

So lets start with the basics. We know that for a Christian, in order to be "saved" or "born again", it is necessary to acknowledge Jesus Christ as the Son of God, the Messiah, our Savior, and of our own free will allow Him to be Lord of our life. That is, as best you know how, you must acknowledge that He died for your sins, redeemed you from the punishment of spiritual death (separation from God for eternity) and offer you eternal life with Him. Once you move to that place He will begin to transform your life.

Beyond this we must then move into areas that I believe we hear little about but which affect us in significant ways. Obviously being forgiven of our past sins is a great relief to us. But what about those people who sinned against us, and whom we need to forgive? What about those things that we need to forgive in ourselves? Things that we hang onto because we've not even thought about how important it is to forgive them? Sometimes we need to forgive ourselves for what we have done to others, things that we have said or done that we now regret. It can be difficult for us to forgive ourselves for our part in the pain that we caused.

I remember vividly driving along the highway in my car when God suddenly brought to mind my mother who had died several years before. I found myself crying and asking her to forgive me for things I had done that I knew were hurtful to her when she was alive. But in the process I also needed to forgive myself for hurting my mother. I had tried to cope with the shame and guilt of hurting my mother by stuffing it away. It wasn't big things but I was feeling that I could have been a better son in caring for her in her later years when she really needed me. I had guilt over making decisions that I had felt were best for me but which were hurtful to her. Now here I was, driving down the highway bawling like a baby asking my mom to forgive me, facing my own guilt and forgiving myself. The sense of freedom was immediate and significant.

Perhaps you realize you have guilt or shame over something you thought had been settled. Maybe you made a bad choice at some point in your life and you have been living with the consequences ever since. Or maybe you have made your own life a lot more difficult than it needed to be. Or you have caused another pain and it grieves you to the core of your being.

Jesus died on the cross in order that your sins could be forgiven. You must forgive both others who have hurt you and sometimes yourself over what you did to other people. If you don't do this you will live with the bondage and baggage of unforgiveness and you are in effect rejecting His gift. You are refusing to appropriate, accept, and live in the reality of the forgiveness He has provided.

THE TRAPS OF UNFORGIVENESS

One of the major keys to freedom from bondage, and growth in intimacy with God, is found in forgiveness. I know this may sound a little extreme at first, but trust me when I say that *most of the ground Satan gains in the lives of Christians is due to unforgiveness.* Obviously, we know we need to forgive others. Scripture makes it clear that forgiveness is required. I would go so far as to say that it is the key to experiencing inner healing. What is inner healing? It is emotional healing that takes place when we deal effectively with areas from our past that continue to plague us in the present.

THE FOUNDATION OF FORGIVENESS

The basis of all our interaction with the issue of forgiveness as Christians is found in the bedrock reality that God has amply, overwhelmingly, undeservedly, and completely forgiven us. Scripture makes this very clear: *In him we have redemption through his blood, the forgiveness of sins, in accordance with the riches of God's grace that he lavished on us with all wisdom and understanding* (Ephesians. 1:7-8). *For he has rescued us from the dominion of darkness and brought us into the kingdom of the Son he loves, in whom we have redemption, the forgiveness of sins* (Colossians. 1:13-14).

Sadly, but not surprisingly, some people find it incomprehensible to accept that they have been forgiven. On one occasion I was ministering at a maximum-security prison and after the teaching was finished I saw this prisoner near the back of the chapel making his way up the aisle towards me. When he was close to me he said; "Can I ask you a question?" "Sure," I replied. He looked at me with apprehension on his face and asked, "When Jesus forgave me of my sins did he forgive me of all of them?" "Yes," I answered. He asked again, "You mean all of them?" I said again, "Yes!" With this stunned look on his face he slowly turned around, and as he walked away I heard him say, "Wow, all of them! I can't believe it. All of them!"

THE RESPONSE GOD SEEKS

Oddly enough, God isn't satisfied with being the only person in the forgiveness business. He expects us to take a play out of His playbook and do a little forgiving ourselves. Actually a lot of it. How much? As much as it takes.

The teachings of Jesus were extraordinary because they were often the opposite of what we naturally think is right. The following quote from the Sermon on the Mount was meant to have a revolutionary effect in our hearts and minds. *You have heard that it was said, "Love your neighbor and hate your enemy." But I tell you: Love your enemies and pray for those who persecute you...*(Matthew 5:43-45).

This was a revolutionary thought. "Love your enemies and pray for those who persecute you!" Are you nuts!? It's their fault I'm in this mess.

IMPRISONED BY THE C.I.A.

If you allow unforgiveness to remain in your life, you will be imprisoned by one of these three traps: Condemnation, Intimidation, and Accusation. An easy way to remember these is the acronym C.I.A.

THE FIRST TRAP: CONDEMNATION

Condemnation means, "To pronounce judgment against or to declare unfit for use." Occasionally in ministry we run into people who feel as if what they have done is so bad that even God will not forgive them. They feel that whatever punishment comes they deserve. Or, in some cases, when they are forgiven they cannot forgive the people who hurt them. Some feel like the woman caught in the act of adultery in John.

Jesus returned to the Mount of Olives, but early the next morning he was back again at the Temple. A crowd soon gathered, and he sat down and taught them. As he was speaking, the teachers of religious law and Pharisees brought a woman they had caught in the act of adultery. They put her in front of the crowd. "Teacher," they said to Jesus, " this woman was caught in the very act of adultery. The Law of Moses says to stone her. What do you say?" They were trying to trap him into saying something they could use against him, but Jesus stooped down and wrote in the dust with his finger. They kept demanding an answer, so he stood up again and said, "All right, stone her. But let those who have never sinned throw the first stones!" Then he stooped down again and wrote in the dust. When the accusers heard this, they slipped away one by one, beginning with the oldest, until only Jesus was left in the middle of the crowd with the woman (John 8: 1-11, NLT)

Obviously, she was being used by the Pharisees to bait Jesus. And, she knew her behavior violated the Law of Moses and just as surely she knew that the penalty of adultery was death. Her accusers were condemning her and they were correct and justified in their condemnation. What do you think she was feeling while standing there? Afraid? Degraded? Guilty? Ashamed? Probably she was experiencing all of these and more. But then after Jesus dealt with her accusers and they left, He turned His attention to her. *"Where are your accusers? Didn't even one of them condemn you?" "No, Lord," she said. And Jesus said, "Neither do I. Go and sin no more"* (John 8:10-11, NLT)

What has just happened to her? Suddenly she is forgiven, free from condemnation. She is no longer facing death. She has been declared not guilty! Just as the Pharisees had a choice when Jesus challenged them, she is faced with a choice:

First, there is the reality of accepting this forgiveness. She may have gone away from there not really able to accept that she was forgiven. She may have been so ashamed and guilty, knowing full well she deserved the punishment of death, that she allowed the enemy to keep her trapped under condemnation even though she had been clearly forgiven by Jesus. If it were totally beyond her that she could be forgiven, Satan would find her an easy target. He whispers things like, "You really haven't been forgiven. Look at what you did! Do you think God could forgive you and love you after what you've done?" Satan loves to trap us in this condemnation.

Her second choice was in how she would handle giving that same forgiveness to her accusers. She needed to release them from what they had just done to her or carry her anger, resentment and bitterness toward them around with her. It could destroy her. It would be easy for her to be bitter. She had been spied on, and then dragged out in front of everybody and embarrassed and degraded. Now the whole village knew about her affair. That bitterness and anger could be easily turned around to keep her under condemnation. The unforgiveness brings the condemnation, because it is sin.

This condemnation can be in the form of words spoken to us by people who are very significant in our lives. Words such as, "You'll never amount to anything; you'll always be a loser." These words are like daggers stuck into our hearts and can be the very words that condemn us to becoming losers and failures. Numerous times we have prayed with people who heard these words from their fathers, mothers or other significant people in their lives and these words have brought condemnation because they believed them and lived as if they were true. They felt "unfit for use."

This is a trap you can work your way out of by understanding who you are in Christ and that you are free from condemnation! *Therefore, there is now no condemnation for those who are in Christ Jesus* (Romans 8:1). Satan knows that if he can keep you from understanding the truth of your forgiveness and who you are in Christ, he can keep you trapped by condemnation.

THE SECOND TRAP: INTIMIDATION

To intimidate means to fill with fear, to coerce, inhibit or discourage by threats. This often happens after you make a commitment. If the enemy can intimidate you he has won a great victory. He will use any means he can, but most often he will use those people around you who are your friends or associates.

The Traps of Unforgiveness

A number of years ago when Wholeness Ministries began there was significant opposition to it. This ministry was birthed with great pain. At that time I was in a traditional Baptist church and the area of physical healing was just beginning to be explored. There wasn't much problem with physical healing but when we began to move into areas of inner healing and deliverance there were problems. During this time I was trying to learn everything I could about healing. I was attending seminars, reading books, and hanging out with people in the healing ministry. We were beginning to see some significant results as we prayed for people. However, it wasn't long before some people in the church began to raise questions about what we were doing. We were accused of manipulating people, of being unscriptural, of being "New Age." This was because of some of the books we were reading and the ways in which the Holy Spirit was manifesting during church services.

My integrity and honesty were attacked. My motives were called into question. I was asked to go before a group in the church and defend what we were doing and answer charges they were making, charges over things I had said or written which were taken completely out of context. Things that were said about us were not true and were deeply wounding to me personally. It was a tough time for my wife and me. We lost some friends that we'd had for years who couldn't understand what we were doing. I found myself angry and resentful at the people who were doing this and I couldn't understand why. I remember sitting by a river complaining to God about all the flack I was getting. I remember saying, "God, why is this happening? All I want to do is pray for people. What's the big deal here? Why can't we just forget about all this hassle over how we're doing what we do and just do the stuff? All I want is for people to get healed."

I found myself becoming angry towards some specific individuals and it was beginning to affect my ministry to people. I even began to question what I was doing. Maybe I was wrong. This intimidated me and I became very careful of what I said and did, because I was afraid of being attacked and having to constantly defend myself. What happened was that these people eventually left the church. As I look back on this entire event I see how easily

Satan was using this to manipulate, divide and destroy people. Because of these accusations, before I could move ahead, I had to later work through some unforgiveness issues with people who had hurt me. What I did by granting this forgiveness was pull the ground right out from under Satan. I released to God those very things Satan was accusing me of - anger, bitterness, and resentment. And God forgave me. If I had allowed Satan to keep me in this trap the ministry we were doing could have very well been destroyed.

Another way Satan will intimidate you is through Scripture. He will use people in positions of authority to quote verses to you. They will say to you, "It says right here in Scripture that we have been rescued from the kingdom of darkness, purchased with his blood and forgiven for all of our sins." Therefore, according to their reasoning, since I have been washed in the blood, all the past is done and I don't need to think about it anymore! This is deadly! This is a trap of the enemy.

While those Scriptures are certainly true, it doesn't mean that we will be exempt from the *consequences* of our sins. This includes both those sins we commit and those sins committed against us. We have churches full of people walking around with anger, hatred, jealousy or bitterness in their lives. And people dealing with addictions and compulsions that keep them from living victorious lives. Most of the hurt that remains in people's lives is hurt which they have not been able to release.

THE THIRD TRAP: ACCUSATION

Accusation means bringing charges against someone. We know from Scripture that Satan is the accuser. *For the Accuser has been thrown down to earth - the one who accused our brothers and sisters before our God day and night* (Revelation 12:10 NLT). How many times does Satan try to stop or destroy us with accusation? He accuses us before God and he accuses us to our face. He will say, "Who do you think you are? You are nothing! You are of no value to God. You don't have any power to overcome that sin. You are such a hypocrite. You call yourself a Christian. How can you be a Christian and do that? How can you feel that way?!"

I was eighteen when my father was killed. I had just graduated from high school. My father was not an alcoholic but on occasion he would go out and come home drunk. One night he went out and didn't come back, so my mom went out looking for him. She found him outside a bar, brought him home and then took him to a hospital after she determined he was indeed seriously hurt. We learned later that he was beaten outside a local bar in the town where we lived. He died a week later from the blows to his head. When this came up for a legal hearing the entire case against the men who had beaten him was dropped because there was not enough evidence to bring them to trial. I felt betrayed by the judicial system. I was angry at the police, the sheriff and the judge. As a result, I began to distrust and rebel against authority, especially anyone associated with the legal system. I felt anger toward my father. My reasoning was that it was his fault that he had gone out, gotten drunk and gotten into a fight that left me without a dad when I needed one badly. I felt abandoned and lonely without my father.

I was angry with him and angry with God for taking him. I couldn't let God love me deeply and intimately, nor could I respond back to Him, because I didn't want to risk getting hurt again. I found it difficult to get very close to other men; thus, most of my friendships were very superficial. I kept a guard on how close I let anyone get to me. It took a number of years before I was able to come to grips with this and let the hurt and pain surface. After I faced it and dealt with it before God, then I could accept God's love and let others who wanted to be friends become close to me. Only after I did this was I able to get on with my life and move into an intimate relationship with God and others. After this happened God was able to use me as a channel of His love to others.

What makes this so significant is that many of those years when I was so guarded I was in full-time ministry. I was supposed to have an intimate relationship with God, I was supposed to be open and loving, I was supposed to know how to help people move into loving relationships through forgiveness. But I had given the enemy ample opportunity to accuse me, which made me pull back because of the anger I was hiding. Remember this, Satan stands before God at any opportunity to accuse you and he takes every opportunity you give him by holding on to unforgiveness.

If we have been trapped by Condemnation, Intimidation or Accusation then we are faced with a question, the answer to which will either keep us trapped or bring us into freedom.

TO FORGIVE OR NOT TO FORGIVE

To forgive those who have caused us great pain is not an easy thing. It goes against our sense of justice. It is not fair. They deserve to be punished. However, Jesus is asking us to forgive others because of His grace and mercy in forgiving us. We deserved to be punished and it wasn't fair to Him that He had to go to the cross on our account, but He was willing to do that. *The Father loves me because I lay down my life that I may have it back again. No one can take my life from me. I lay down my life voluntarily. For I have the right to lay it down when I want to and also the power to take it up again. For my Father has given me this command* (John 10:17-18 NLT).

THERE ARE SOME IMPORTANT THINGS TO KNOW ABOUT FORGIVENESS

To forgive doesn't necessarily mean that we are going to forget. Our past is our past. But it does mean that we are not going to hold the offense against that person any longer. We are going to release it and let it go. When true forgiveness takes place, the feelings of hurt and anger associated with that offense will be gone.

Forgiving is not pretending that the offense didn't matter. Part of genuine forgiveness is to face the hurt and to realize that even after you forgive you may have to continue to live with the consequences of that offense.

A number of years ago I was deeply wounded by a friend. He did not even know that what he said and did caused me hurt and pain. I internalized my feelings and excused his behavior by saying such things as, "That's just the way he is, so get over it." I found that I began to feel a wall going up in my relationship with him. Although in my time of prayer I had forgiven him, when I thought about the event all those hurt feelings would surface.

About three years after this happened I was on vacation with my wife. Early one morning I was sitting out on the deck having coffee and listening to some music. Suddenly this friend's favorite song came on and I felt as if I had been punched in the stomach. I started sobbing and all those feelings came to the surface. I knew I had to release them, forgive him and let God heal the hurt. The next time I saw him, though I remembered the event, those hurt, angry feelings were not there and I felt as if the wall had been broken down.

Forgiving does not necessarily mean the person is entirely off the hook. Sometimes people find it difficult to forgive because they feel that the person is getting away with the offense. It seems unfair. People have said to me, "You have no idea what they did to me. I can't let them off that easily." But I say to them, "You are releasing them from your anger into God's hands. God, who is much wiser and far more capable of handling things than we are, is left in charge. Trust God to deal with it."

Forgiveness is a choice. It is a crisis of the will. It is also a crisis of trust and obedience. It is our Lord, our Master, it is Jesus Himself who is commanding us to forgive. Would He command us to do something we were incapable of doing? Do we trust Him to have our best interest at heart as He gives us this command?

Forgiving benefits both the forgiver and the forgiven. It's been said that, "As long as people are angry at each other, they are chained to each other." We are emotionally chained to those we refuse to forgive. We are literally dragging them around with us emotionally. But the act of forgiving sets both them and us free. Note that at the end of the parable of the unforgiving servant (Matthew 18:23-35) *both* servants end up in jail.

A pastor recently referred to carrying bitterness as "emotional suicide." In Job, a bitter person is described as, *"you who tear yourself to pieces in your anger"* (Job 18:4). The fact that anger harms the person who is angry ("tears him to pieces") is not just a Biblical truth but a widely accepted psychological and medical fact. In one of her many syndicated columns Ann Landers printed this little gem of truth, "Anger is like acid. It does more harm to the object in which it is stored than to the object on which it is poured."[1]

The fact is that the person you are angry with may not even be aware of your anger. They may have no idea and suffer no ill effects of your anger at all, while it eats away at you daily.

For over nineteen years I was on staff of a large church. As I mentioned earlier, I came under attack by some in the church and felt abandoned by my immediate boss, the senior pastor. The final result of this situation was my decision to resign. When I left, I knew there was some unfinished business with him, but I was not willing to deal with it because I felt that nothing would change, so why bother.

He eventually retired and I lost complete track of him, but I noticed that whenever his name was mentioned I immediately felt resentment towards him. A number of years passed and occasionally our paths crossed, but I was not comfortable around him and did not care to have any relationship with him. Well, God had other plans for me.

There came a point when God said, "I want you to contact him and deal with this bitterness and hurt that you have over the way he treated you." My response was, "I don't know where he is and don't know what to say." I'm not sure how this happened but in a short time I had an address. So I wrote him a letter explaining how I felt towards him and that I had forgiven him. I assumed that was the end of it and we would both go merrily our way. NOT! He called me after receiving the letter and we both talked through how we felt. When we were done I knew that all my anger and bitterness were gone. This was verified for me when I saw him the next time. Whereas in the past I would have ignored him, I was actually glad to see him and thoroughly enjoyed our time together. The following verse was brought to life for me. *Do not judge, and you will not be judged. Do not condemn, and you will not be condemned. Forgive, and you will be forgiven* (Luke 6:37).

Even though you understand that your own personal emotional healing depends on your willingness to forgive, it may still be a very difficult thing for you to do. But if you are willing and ask the Holy Spirit to help you, He will help you get to the point where you can forgive. Jesus is our example. From the cross, He said, "*Father, forgive them, for they do not know what they are doing*" (Luke 23:34).

THE SERIOUS BUSINESS OF FORGIVENESS

Escaping all the traps and snares of unforgiveness is not easy. If it were easy, it wouldn't be such a huge issue in the ministry of inner healing! In my years of ministry I have discovered that *most Christians are entirely unaware of how much bitterness they still harbor over things that happened to them in the past*. That's because most of the time we don't experience this bitterness as a clearly defined or obvious emotion on the surface of our consciousness. We say we have moved on and that we have gotten over it. We boast in our resilience, shrugging it off as the sort of thing that sometimes happens, claiming that we are too tough-skinned to cry over a little spilt milk. We are like a friend of mine whose stock reply when anyone asked about his parents divorce was, "Don't make a big deal about it. I'm fine. I learned to cope – I dealt with it pretty well. I don't think it really affected me that much."

"I don't think it really affected me that much." These, my friends, are not the words of forgiveness. They are the words of denial. Someone who is in denial will never experience true healing for the obvious reason that they do not believe there is a wound that needs healing in the first place. But just because we aren't consciously dwelling on our bitterness, or being self-aware enough to label it as such, does not mean that we are somehow going to be exempt from feeling the full effects of our bondage.

It is my experience that unforgiveness is at the root of so many of our spiritual, emotional, and physical problems that we must never rule out the high probability that when we are in some state of undefined and inexplicable distress, unforgiveness may well be to blame.

So, why don't we spend more time looking there? Why isn't there more emphasis in the church on dealing with unforgiveness? Don't we understand how important forgiveness truly is? Of course we do. And therein lies the problem.

As Christians we all know that forgiveness is a pretty big deal. Our only hope for salvation is in God's forgiveness. His willingness to forgive our sin and rebellion is at the very heart of the Christian faith. And we are also all aware of Jesus' emphatic promise that we will not be able to access our Heavenly Father's forgiveness so long as we refuse to be forgiving ourselves. The promised forgiveness that we so desperately depend upon apparently comes from a clause: Forgive, or you will not be forgiven – no excuses, no extenuating circumstances, just forgive…end of discussion.

For a Christian forgiving is a big deal…which is precisely why nobody wants to admit that they haven't done it! After all, based on what Jesus said, if I admit to harboring bitterness and unforgiveness, am I admitting that I'm still not really forgiven by God in this one area? If I suddenly admit to having not forgiven my father, for example, for something that happened thirty years ago, what does that say about how I have been living all this time?

This whole obsession with keeping up appearances is pure foolishness, because there is no shame in uncovering your issues of unforgiveness in order that you might pursue deeper levels of healing and wholeness. Sure, it can be humbling to admit that you are not yet completely holy and perfect, not yet exactly like Jesus. But everyone around you could have told you that already, so there is no harm in admitting it to yourself!

Now, in some circles an easy forgiveness being preached, an over-all, general forgiveness that misses the importance of what I cannot emphasize enough: rooting out every last drop of bitterness and unforgiveness is something that is vitally important to God. He wants more than a one-time, blanket "I forgive everyone who ever hurt me in the past" kind of prayer. He also wants us to walk in true forgiveness – not just lip service, not just saying that we forgive someone – but the kind of forgiveness that cleanses us from all the old festering bitterness. He wants us to take this seriously, because He takes it seriously.

Remember the story I told earlier? Of my associate's father, who was led to forgive a relative over whom he'd experienced anger and bitterness many years before? With all the things God might have wanted to say to His servant before leaving this Earth, He chose to bring attention to this old, old issue of unforgiveness from his distant past. I can't tell you for absolute certain why this was, but the inference was unmistakable: his father needed to forgive his sister-in-law while he was still here, still in the body. As good and as righteous a Christ-follower as my associate's father was, God didn't want him coming home until the unforgiveness was settled.

THE PATH TO FORGIVENESS

So please hear me when I say that this issue is big. The steps to healing the wounds of bitterness, and escaping the traps of unforgiveness, are helpful and life-giving in your own personal walk to freedom from a bondage that you may have been under for years. Let's consider these steps.

First, you must make the decision that you want to forgive and be set free.

This is a crucial first step. You cannot force this or do this just because someone says you need to. It is absolutely necessary that this decision be made before you proceed to the next step.

Then, pray and ask the Holy Spirit to bring to mind people and events, that He knows are the roots of the anger in your heart. It is highly likely, especially if there are a lot of issues there, that everything will not be revealed at once but over a period of time. Deal with whomever or whatever He shows you. Be on the alert for things you haven't thought about in years to suddenly come to mind. If something that comes is painful, allow the pain. If you feel like weeping, then weep.

Identify specifically the offense for which you need to forgive a person. This is a crucial step. For example, don't just say, "I forgive you, dad," but "I forgive you dad for not being there when I needed you. I felt so rejected and that I was not very important to you at all." Being specific helps us to identify the wound, and that helps as we pray for healing.

We may have to forgive the same person for many different things. Or we may on different occasions have to forgive the same offense, especially if the same offense is continuing to occur. *Then Peter came to Jesus and asked, "Lord, how many times shall I forgive my brother when he sins against me? Up to seven times?" Jesus answered, "I tell you, not seven times, but seventy times seven"* (Matthew 18:21–22).

We will never be done forgiving. Always being willing to take the path of forgiveness is necessary to staying healthy physically, emotionally and spiritually.

It is important to be honest before God in regards to how you feel about the person or the event. God knows it all anyway, but he desires you to verbalize it. Nothing is going to surprise him, but you need to get it out and lay it before him. David Seamands says, "There is nothing you can share out of the agonizing hurts and depths and hates and rages of your soul that God has not heard. There is nothing you can take to Him that He will not understand. He will receive you with love and grace."[2] *Nothing in all creation is hidden from God's sight. Everything is uncovered and laid bare before the eyes of him to whom we must give account* (Hebrews: 4:13).

At this point you must forgive the offense. It may be helpful to get alone in a place where no one can hear you and talk out loud to the person you need to forgive just as if he or she were in the room with you. Tell the person that you forgive him and specifically what the offense is that you are forgiving. If the person has died you can still forgive him; in fact, you must. You are still alive, and have been carrying the burden of unforgiveness. The act of forgiveness finally frees you. Obviously, we cannot repent and ask people to forgive us after they are gone, but you can ask God to forgive you. Praying out loud will help you in the future to remember that as an act of your will, you did forgive the person. You made it official.

A crucial part of this process is that you must pray and ask God to forgive you for holding unforgiveness in your heart. He will forgive you. *If we confess our sins, he is faithful and just to forgive us our sins and purify us from all unrighteousness* (1 John 1:9).

You must also forgive yourself. One of the most difficult things for people to do is to forgive themselves for their part of their pain. Maybe you realize you share some of the guilt in regards to an offense for which you have forgiven another. Perhaps you have been suffering the consequences of one poor choice you made earlier in your life and you can't forgive yourself for that choice. Maybe you see now how your own decisions have made your own life a lot tougher than it needed to be. Maybe you now realize how you caused another pain, and it grieves you deeply. But Jesus died on the cross in order that your sins could be forgiven. So you are now free to forgive yourself.

MAD AT GOD - WHO, ME?!

One often-overlooked piece of this process is dealing with your anger towards God. It is necessary to face this issue, though Christians find it very difficult to do so. What are those things you are holding against God Himself?

In some cases we harbor anger against God for something we feel he should have done, but didn't, or something we believe He did do, and shouldn't have done. What do we do with that anger?

It is quite common when a tragedy strikes such as the 911 attacks, or Hurricane Katrina, or some other significant disaster, for people to automatically say something like, "God, how could you let this happen?" Or when it's more personal such as losing a loved one we respond with, "God why didn't you prevent this?" So we blame Him and this blame can easily turn into bitterness toward God, serious baggage that we carry around for years. This, of course, affects our relationship with Him and others.

It is necessary to face this kind of baggage. Many Christians find it difficult even to admit that they are angry toward God. What are those things you are holding against God Himself? Neil Anderson teaches that, "Technically, we don't forgive God because He cannot commit any sin of commission or omission. But you need to specifically renounce false expectations and thoughts about God and agree to release any anger you have toward Him."[3]

It is hard for us to admit that we hold things against God, but we do. We blame Him for how things have gone. Sometimes we are angry about how He made us, or the parents He gave us, or we believed He would do something and He let us down.

You need to identify the issues you have with God. You need to ask forgiveness for your anger towards Him. You need to accept that forgiveness.

Then comes the point when you need to pray for healing. Forgiving is like lancing a boil. It allows all the infection and pus to come out and then you treat it with medicine to bring healing. Once you have forgiven someone - whether it is another person, yourself, or God - it is time to pray and ask Jesus to heal the wound. Ask His Holy Spirit to fill the voids in your life, to bring comfort, to fill you with love and the reality of the acceptance and forgiveness of Jesus. The healing process may take some time, but welcome and rejoice in it.

Begin to pray for the people you have forgiven. If they don't know the Lord, pray that they will come to know Him. Pray for blessings for them. Pray that Jesus will help you see them through His eyes.

A WORD OF CAUTION

We need to be very careful about approaching the person we have forgiven. It is one thing to go to someone to repent and ask their forgiveness for something you've done, and quite another to confront someone with the fact that you are forgiving them. If the person is unaware of how you feel, it is best to deal with it between you and the Lord and leave it there. If it is someone from whom you have been estranged and you would like to reconcile, pray extensively about it first.

It doesn't aid in reconciliation to approach someone and say, for example, "I forgive you for being an insensitive jerk." A much better approach is to confess that you've been angry and have asked God's forgiveness and would like to ask the person's. Let him know that he means a lot to you and you would like to reconcile. He may or may not forgive you or apologize to you. Be prepared for that and let it go. As we are set free from the pain in our own life, we don't want to inflict pain on someone else in the process.

Forgiveness is part of the Christian walk. It is a wonderful provision for us that allows us to be free in the mercy and grace of Jesus.

A LOOK IN THE MIRROR
(Healing The Wounded Self-Image)

In our world today we have support groups for just about everything. We are a wounded people. We may have grown up in families where we were deeply wounded by things that were said or done to us. We have gone to schools where we may have been embarrassed by our looks, or our lack of athletic ability. Maybe we've come to accept that were not really of much value or that we don't have a great deal to give. That's exactly where the enemy would like to keep you.

WHAT DO YOU SEE?

When you look at yourself in the mirror, what do you see? Do you like what you see? At some point you may have said, "I hate myself! I don't like my nose, legs, etc. I'm not wanted. I'm so clumsy, I can't do anything right. I'm not good enough to be accepted and forgiven by God. I wish I were a boy/girl." If you have, statements like this are typical of someone with a deeply wounded self-image. If someone asked you, "How do you feel about yourself?" Would you be able to honestly say, "I love myself"? Or would you, like many of us, confess that there are things about you that you do not like and would change if you could?

Charles Kraft, in his book *Deep Wounds, Deep Healing*, believes that the roots of self-rejection in many people lay in the knowledge they had before birth that their parents did not want them.

"We have found when praying for an individual that sometimes during prayer they will express that they knew they were not wanted even before their birth. They felt rejection and abandonment in the mother's womb. They felt afraid and were fearful of life. We know that a child developing in the womb feels and experiences what the mother feels and experiences. We know the child senses things like fear and rejection. So it is of no surprise when we minister to people that we find these feelings go back to before their actual birth."[1]

SATAN'S STRATEGY

Though we cannot blame Satan for our weaknesses and failures, we have to recognize that he lurks in the background, ready and waiting to take advantage of whatever is there to harass and, if possible, destroy us. "SATAN'S GREATEST PSYCHOLOGICAL WEAPON IS A GUT-LEVEL FEELING OF INFERIORITY, INADEQUACY, AND LOW SELF-WORTH."[2]

We hear messages that come from various sources that say: "You are worthless! You can't do anything right! You're a mistake!" But the Bible presents us with a very different view. When God created us, he positioned us above the angels, including Satan himself. Thus Satan is jealous and angry. He especially attacks those things he cannot have such as our creativity and our ability to procreate. We read in Psalms, *For you made us only a little lower than God and you crowned us with glory and honor* (Psalm 8:4-5, NLT).

He is envious of the position God has given us, just a bit lower than God Himself. Most translations have rendered this "a little lower than angels" but the actual word "angels" is "Elohim," which is translated God. Only human beings are created in the image of God. Only we have been given the privilege by God to procreate others in His image.

GOD'S PLAN

The Bible constantly affirms that human beings are valuable in God's sight. We were created in God's image with intellectual abilities, the capacity to communicate, to procreate, the freedom to make choices, the knowledge of right and wrong, and the responsibility to administer and rule over the rest of creation.

Then God said, "Let us make man in our image, our likeness, and let them rule over the fish of the sea and the birds of the air, over the livestock, over all the earth and over all the creatures that move along the ground." So God created man in His own image, in the image of God he created him; male and female he created them (Genesis 1:26).

We read in Psalms, You put us in charge of everything you made, giving us authority over all things, the sheep and the cattle and all the wild animals, the birds in the sky, the fish in the sea, and everything that swims the oceans currents" (Psalm 8:6-8, NLT).

So we are made in God's image, we are positioned just below God, and we have been placed here to rule over all of creation. If this were not affirming enough in regards to your value, listen to what God says in Jeremiah, *Before I formed you in the womb I knew you...* (Jeremiah 1:5). God doesn't make mistakes! He formed you and He likes what He formed.

Do you think God would have sent His only son to die for us if we were not special? He also sent angels to guard us, the Holy Spirit to guide us and the Scriptures to teach us. We are valuable enough to Him that we will spend eternity with Him in a place prepared for us in heaven.

SATAN'S PLAN

Satan has a strategic plan to keep us from becoming what God intended us to be.

He tempts people to obey him and does his best to keep them from responding to God's plan of salvation by blinding them to the truth of God's Word. He continues to tempt believers to sin. His assault against us never stops and even when we confess our sin, he tries to keep us from feeling forgiven.

How many times have you dealt with this one? Satan loves to say to you, "Could God really forgive you for that? What you did was so bad that He will never forgive you." Does that sound familiar?

He also plants lies in our minds. Especially lies concerning our identity before God. Satan encourages teachings that say we are worthless, inadequate or evil. Whatever he can do to make us feel useless and contemptible, he will do.

Before You Get Here

As a young man I remember hearing sermons that continually told me about the horrors of hell. They emphasized that many of those things I wanted to do were sin. Of course to me they were all the things that were fun. I was told that even if I thought about those things I was bad. They made certain I understood that God was going to get me if I did anything wrong. I didn't see myself as a person of value to God, but rather one that He was continually watching; waiting to catch me doing something wrong. I grew up thinking that God was there to spoil my fun. With that kind of background in church, plus what was happening in my life as I was entering adolescence, no wonder my self-esteem was in the toilet.

In my family the men were all hunters. I didn't particularly like to hunt but it was the "manly" thing to do. My father, grandfather, brother, uncles, etc. all hunted, so in order to spend "manly" time with the guys, I had to hunt. I will never forget my first hunting experience. We were out on the opening day of dove season. I had in my hands a 20-gauge shotgun. Suddenly a dove came flying over my head. I shot and hit the bird and when we all ran over to where the bird was laying on the ground I saw that I had merely wounded it, not killed it. The dove was flopping around on the ground looking up at me with these eyes that seemed to say, "Why did you do that to me? I've not done anything to hurt you." The men were all congratulating me on what a great hunter I was going to be. On the outside I was smiling, looking real proud of myself, but on the inside I was crying. I felt awfully sad over what I had just done.

I vividly remember my junior high and high school days. My family was very involved in church, so not only was I dealing with all this hell-fire and brimstone teaching but also my hormones were kicking in and I was a physical, emotional mess. In school, when it came time to choose up teams for sports like baseball, basketball or whatever; I was always one of the last ones as the team captains argued over who would have to take me on their team. Talk about feeling inadequate. I was short, skinny and uncoordinated.

It wasn't until the latter part of my college years that I discovered there were two sports that I could do well. They were snow skiing and sailing. I became an avid snow skier. I had found a sport that I was very good at. What that did for my self-esteem was significant.

It was also during these years that I begin to hear that I was of value to God, of great worth and significance. I was actually receiving positive input and feeling good about myself.

WHY IS IT IMPORTANT TO KNOW YOUR TRUE IDENTITY?

There was a popular teaching during the 1800's that continually focused on our sinfulness before God. In this teaching we were portrayed as needing to grovel before God begging Him to please listen to us, even though we were too wretched to be in His presence. There are so many things wrong with this teaching. Let's start with the concept that we are wretched creatures that don't even deserve to be in the presence of God. Think about this: do you feel that way about your kids? We are His kids! I don't take lightly the fact that we can actually be in His presence because of what Jesus has done. But God, like a loving human father, wants intimate relationship with us. He wants us to know how valued and loved we are., and to understand that we are His children, heirs to all that Jesus has inherited. Obviously, we need to understand who it is that we are in the presence of and go in to Him with reverence and humility. There are also times when we go into His presence dancing and singing. And there are times when He wants us to run into the throne room and jump up into His lap. But Satan would have us view God as this harsh, imposing figure, waiting to come down on us, when in fact that is not true.

We were also taught that when we came before God to pray, our prayers were often little more than petitions begging God to please listen to us, even though we were so undeserving. Many of our prayers were prefaced with, "Please God" or "If it be your will God." Prayer was not seen as a conversation with a loving God anxious to listen and answer our prayers.

HOW DOES A NEGATIVE SELF-IMAGE AFFECT US?

Earlier I asked, "When you look at yourself in the mirror are you pleased with what God made?" Do you like your body, your ears, your nose, and your feet? Are you able to accept yourself as you are and thank Him for how He made you? Or do you think something like: "My ears are too big, my nose is too big, I'm too fat, too skinny, too tall, too short." Or perhaps you see yourself as too sensitive, too weak, or stupid.

I remember when a young man came to talk with me and asked for prayer. As he shared what was going on with him I realized that one of his biggest problems was a very poor self-image. He expressed to me all the things he didn't like about himself. Most of what he said had to do with how he saw himself physically. He was not happy with his body and the way God had put him together. At that time he was in high school. The peer pressure to have the perfect body can be especially intense during those adolescent years.

As I listened to him I felt prompted to say, "I want you to go home, get alone by yourself in front of a mirror. Take all your clothes off so that you are standing there completely naked. Then start at the top of your head and begin to thank God for every part, working your way down to your feet."

I know this may sound a bit strange to tell someone, but I felt that it was exactly what he needed to do to begin to understand why God made him that way and to begin to like himself. When he came back the next week he told me how it went. He said, "I did what you asked me to do. At first it was very hard and I did not want to do it. As I started at the top of my head I was mostly complaining about the size of my ears or my nose and the shape of my head. But as I began to thank God for all the various parts, my emotions went from anger to tears of joy and gratitude. By the time I reached my feet I was excited and rejoicing over the way God had put me together. I am totally happy with myself!"

If your response is, "Well that's prideful," let me remind you that God is very clear that we are to love ourselves. We are even commanded to love our neighbor as we love ourselves. I've since watched this young man grow into a wonderful husband and father who is great fun to be around and radiates a love and humility that reflect his understanding of God's love for him.

I suspect if most of us were honest we would admit to not being happy with the way God made us. That negative self-image affects our relationship with God in a number of ways.

For example, you may look in the mirror and say to yourself, "This is the best He can do? If this is an example of His creativity and His love, then I'm not very impressed. How can I believe He loves me and how can I trust Him?" Perhaps this is you. You want to really trust God but you just can't stir up enough faith to do so. This is often a result of a deep rejection of self, which overlooks what God is preparing to accomplish in and through your life.

If you had said to me 25 years ago that someday I would be traveling around the world, teaching leaders and praying for healing, and doing street evangelism in Eastern Europe, I would have said, "NO WAY." Why? One: I really didn't want to do this and, two: I wasn't sure I could trust God.

A FATHER TRYING TO TEACH TRUST

A little boy was afraid of the dark. One night his father told him to go out to the back porch and bring him a bucket. The little boy turned to his father and said, "Daddy, I don't want to go out there. It's dark." The father smiled reassuringly at his son. "You don't have to be afraid of the dark," he explained. Jesus is out there. He'll look after you and protect you." The little boy looked at his father real hard and asked, "Are you sure he's out there?" "Yes, I'm sure," the father replied. "He is everywhere, and he is always ready to help you when you need him." The little boy thought about that for a minute and then went to the back door and cracked it a little. Peering out into the darkness, he called, "Jesus! If you're out there, would you please hand me the bucket?"[3]

When we reject what God has created, we may begin to feel we have been cheated in life. We can develop the attitude that God owes us something. Also, if we don't like what God has created, it hinders our response to others and others' responses to us. This affects our ability to build genuine friendships.

Further, if we don't like ourselves we attempt to compensate for our deficiencies by trying to achieve goals, which we hope will bring acceptance and approval from others. I felt strongly that when I grew up I wanted to be rich, have a respected position, power and lots of stuff! That's what I felt was needed for me to be of value, to be somebody.

A couple of years out of college I was offered a job as Director of Personnel for a large multi-national company based in California. I had a large office, private secretary, nice salary and access to all the "good things" in life. The company had a private jet, a yacht, a Rolls Royce, a large expense account, and a beautiful spread up in the mountains of northern California. All these perks were owned by the company but they were all available for me to enjoy. In my mind, as a young man, I was at the top of my game.

Part of what I was doing because of my rejection of self was putting an overemphasis on clothes and possessions. When this happens people are really saying, "Don't look at me, look at my stuff!"

However, I also learned that in the corporate world there was a steep price to be paid for all this. For this particular corporation, it was all about the bottom line. There was little concern for how people's lives were affected by the way business was conducted. I watched as men who had given up everything to come and work for this company suddenly be dismissed, losing all they had. Values like integrity, honesty and morality were in short supply.

I remember vividly sitting at my desk one day looking around the office at all the trappings when I heard God speak to me and ask me a question that was the start of my journey out of the corporate world. He asked, "Michael are you willing to give your life for this?" My immediate answer was "NO!"

Many years later as I reflected on that experience I realized that God put me in that position as a very young man, to let me work to a point where I had most of what I wanted. Then He revealed to me how empty that was. He started to show me those things that are of real value and that His approval of me was not based on what I had but on who I was. His Beloved!

SYMPTOMS OF THE PROBLEM

Many of us have negative feelings towards our bodies or parts of our bodies. Rarely are the cultural standards for the size and shape of our bodies attained. Think for just a minute. What comes across from the media as the kind of body we are supposed to have? How many of us have that body? And what about how we are expected to present ourselves in public? We are surrounded on television by sparkly personalities, smart articulate people, many who are very talented, gracious and have a great and quick sense of humor. It is easy to feel that we don't measure up.

Many have a sense of shame for even existing. It could come from a mother who was ashamed to be pregnant. I prayed once with a Catholic priest whose mother became pregnant with him before she was married. He has dealt with issues of shame and blame for years. Trying to please and make his mother happy was what drove him. He felt ashamed when he needed help or when he expressed his emotions.

Some people don't like the name they've been given. It doesn't fit who they are. Sometimes it's the name given by parents, other times it's a nickname or a label that we were given by relatives or peers and it stuck with us. Such names as Shorty, Airhead, Redneck, Wingnut or Brainiac can all be names or labels that we have and are not happy with but we are stuck with, at least until we can make an effort to change them. When I was growing up I grew to dislike my name, Michael, because it's what my mother always called me when I was in trouble. I wanted to be called Mike, especially when I entered junior high school. For some reason, the name Michael seemed so weak and Mike seemed somehow more strong and manly. Later when I began to understand who I was in Christ, and learned that Michael meant, "Who is like God," I decided it was okay to be called Michael.

It is not unusual for people to wish they were someone else. This is often someone who looks more attractive. How many of you want to look like someone who you think is uglier than you are? We want to be someone we look up to, someone who is better in sports or music, etc. This can erode our self-esteem if we don't come to grips with it.

There are many ways we try to escape feelings of worthlessness. These can be such things as substance abuse, or athletics, overeating, watching TV, even religion. Some of us at our core don't like ourselves so we use our religion as an addict uses drugs.

We can so dislike ourselves that we curse the parts we don't like. In his book *I Give You Authority*, Dr. Charles Kraft tells the story of a woman who came for prayer because of lumps on her breasts. The Lord revealed she had put a curse on her breasts. It turns out she was abused as a teenager and the abuse focused on her breasts. Dr. Kraft had her pray: "In the name of Jesus, I renounce any curse I have put on myself, or some part of me," and the lumps went away.[4]

If we can't accept ourselves, we believe others can't accept us either, unless we do something to win their approval. Some feel people will never care about them unless they do something significant. Some feel that what love they did receive as children was always conditional. It was based on what they did not who they were. The praise that came was focused on performance, not personhood.

I remember praying with a man who was by all outward appearances happy and successful. But as we talked he shared with me that he felt he could never do enough to please his father. If he worked hard and earned all A's in school his father's response was, "Why didn't you get A+?" If he built some little project to bring home and show him, dad would always point out the flaws.

Why are there some people who always seem to be in trouble? They have a way of doing things that provoke people to anger. Since their low self-esteem keeps them from seeking positive attention, they settle for negative attention. They will do whatever it takes to get noticed.

People who don't like themselves are often negative and critical of anyone who has achieved anything. That's because almost anything they try turns out bad. They see themselves as losers; consequently, they act like losers and turn out to be losers.

HOW TO DEAL WITH OUR WOUNDEDNESS

We must never forget that we are at war. We are in a battle ...*against the wicked spiritual forces in the heavenly world* (Ephesians 6:12). We may find it difficult to even believe that there is a spirit world intent on destroying us but that doesn't change the fact that Satan and his minions are out to do anything they can to stop us or even kill us. Satan hates your guts. You are not just a bit of a bother to him. He is envious and jealous of your position with God and hates the fact that we are made in the image of God. His game plan is to try anything he can to destroy you.

A Look in the Mirror

I was speaking at The Tabernacle in Melbourne, Florida and knew that the evening was going to be a significant one. Earlier in the afternoon I was down at the beach wading in the surf when a strong wave knocked me down. Every time I tried to get up another one hit me. Not only was I being slammed into this rough, gravely sand but I was being drug out farther with each wave. I was scraped and beat up and losing my strength. I'm not normally concerned around the ocean but I was unable to get back up on my feet and it was beginning to scare me. I don't exactly know how this happened but the next thing I know is that a wave picked me up and threw me out on the beach. So there I lay, bruised and worn out with about five pounds of rocks and sand in my swimsuit. I crawled back to the room thinking, I'm not sure if I can give this talk tonight or not. When I was talking to the Lord I asked Him, "Why did that happen?" He said, "Satan was trying to stop you!"

Though this is an example of something Satan used in the physical world, he will usually attack us with words that are abusive, with accusations, or condemnation, and out and out lies. He will take any opportunity to influence people around us to hurt us or even kill us. I am amazed as I travel around at the number of people who don't have a clue that they are in a war. Some will say that we don't need to spend time focused on Satan and his schemes; we just need to know God. I read a quote made by General George S. Patton that said, "No good general goes into battle without a thorough understanding of the enemy. To do so is presumptuous and stupid."[5] I believe we do need to know about him and understand he is always on the prowl to destroy us. I don't believe we must spend a great deal of our time focused on him but neither should we ignore him. Many think that if we ignore him he will go away.

We also need to remember the protection that is ours by virtue of Whose we are. Stop going to places where your worth and value are constantly attacked. Stop hanging around people who are always negative and stop associating more than necessary with people who wound you. Stop thinking of yourself as a loser or someone who cannot do anything right. You are a child of the king, a Prince or Princess with immense value.

Why is it so important for us to know this, to know God's heart for us? It is crucial for our survival! We are heading into a time when our identity as believers could be very costly. Your understanding of the depth of love God has for you may very well determine your ability to stand through this and stay strong. Your sense of personal worth comes from knowing who you are.

YOU MUST HEAR THIS. You are not a mistake! Conception is not simply a physical, human act. Only God can give the life that courses through our physical bodies. And he was not surprised at our conception; He affirmed it by granting us life. From His perspective, you were not an accident. Don't let anyone tell you you're a mistake!

Quit the stinkin' thinkin'. If you think you're a loser you are going to act like a loser. If you continually talk down to yourself you are going to become what you think you are. If you have bought into thinking negative thoughts about yourself you have to bring those thoughts into captivity and change the way you think.

For though we live in the world, we do not wage war as the world does. The weapons we fight with are not the weapons of the world. On the contrary, they have divine power to demolish strongholds. We demolish arguments and every pretension that sets itself up against the knowledge of God, and we take captive every thought to make it obedient to Christ (2 Corinthians 10:3-5).

In Scripture Satan is portrayed as the father of all lies. The human mind is his chief battleground. In Ephesians 6:10-18, believers are instructed to put on the full Armor of God in fighting the enemy, including the Helmet of Salvation, The Sword of the Spirit which is the Word of God, and covering all with prayer. These are three vital elements focusing directly on one's thought-life. Thoughts are usually the controlling influence on one's emotions and will.

We often focus on circumstances, but circumstances themselves do not affect us as much as what we think, expect, and decide to do about those circumstances. We can look at our circumstances and think that we are stuck and will never be able to change, but history shows us that is not necessarily the case. We may think that because we were born into a poor family we will always be poor or we will never be very smart because our parents weren't very smart.

John Maxwell, in his book *Developing The Leader Within You*, said: "Many great people began life in the poorest and most humble of homes, with little education and no advantages. Thomas Edison was a newsboy on trains. Andrew Carnegie started work at $4 a month, John D. Rockefeller at $6 a week. The remarkable thing about Abraham Lincoln was not that he was born in a log cabin, but that he got out of the log cabin. Demosthenes, the greatest orator of the ancient world, stuttered! The first time he tried to make a public speech, he was laughed off the rostrum. Julius Caesar was an epileptic. Napoleon was of humble parentage and far from being a born genius (he stood forty-sixth in his class at the Military Academy in a class of sixty-five). Beethoven was deaf, as was Thomas Edison. Charles Dickens was lame; so was Handel. Homer was blind; Plato was a hunchback; Sir Walter Scott was paralyzed."[6]

Scripture says that we have been given the mind of Christ. Try to see yourself as He sees you. For who has known the mind of the Lord that he may instruct him? But we have the mind of Christ (1 Corinthians 2:16).

HOW DO I QUIT THE STINKIN' THINKIN'?

First, ask the Holy Spirit to reveal thoughts that need to be changed and renewed.

Then ask the Spirit to bring to mind when that thought began. If it involved wounding by another, then begin to forgive that person or persons. This may be easy to do, or it may require some extensive time in prayer and forgiveness.

If you sincerely desire change, then you must begin to do those things that will bring about change. I have discovered that one of the most valuable ways I can spend part of my time is to discipline myself to sit quietly with Him. The purpose of this is not that I might hear something from God, or receive some great insight or wisdom concerning a problem I'm facing. But rather, it is to just enjoy being with Him. That is so much better than trying to live like a joyful Christian while carrying around the baggage of a poor self-image. I believe when we begin to fully understand how valuable we are in God's sight, who we are in Christ, and to honestly face the hurts we have, we will begin a journey towards wholeness that will change our lives!

I WILL NEVER

BREAKING INNER VOWS

"I will never be vulnerable again!" "I will never be like that person…!" Have you ever found yourself saying this or something similar? Of course you have, because we all say these things at some point in our lives. The problem is that we do not understand that what we have done is set ourselves up by making an inner vow. That inner vow is a declaration that binds you to what you have just spoken.

This topic is seldom talked about and typically does not come up in conversation unless you are in counseling with someone or in a ministry session with people who are trying to help you deal with hurts and wounds from the past. Even then, it often goes undetected as we minister to people in the area of Inner Healing. I have found myself at times trying to figure out why some people refuse to change a particular way of thinking or behaving. I have been in prayer appointments with people who keep coming back to me for the same issues.

Why is it that some compulsive behaviors are incredibly difficult to change? One reason may be that an inner vow has been made which was spoken perhaps years ago and forgotten. I was fascinated when I first heard about inner vows and became intrigued as I watched during times of prayer with people how much freedom they received when these inner vows were recognized and broken.

In the dictionary a vow is defined as follows: "a solemn promise or declaration….by which a person is bound to an act, service, or condition."[1] Examples of typical vows would be, "I swear to tell the truth, the whole truth…", "I_____ take thee _____, to have and to hold..." These are vows we are familiar with and are positive vows. Unfortunately most vows we make are not positive and have negative consequences.

In Scripture we see reference to vows and oaths.

> *Above all, my brothers, do not swear - not by heaven or by earth or by anything else. Let your "Yes" be yes, and your "No" be no, or you will be condemned (James 5:12).*

> *Again, you have heard that it was said to the people long ago, "Do not break your oath, but keep the oaths you have made to the Lord." But I tell you, Do not swear at all; either by heaven, for it is God's throne, or by the earth, for it is his footstool; or by Jerusalem, for it is the city of the Great King. And do not swear by your head, for you cannot make even one hair white or black. Simply let your Yes be Yes, and your No, No, anything beyond this comes from the evil one (Matthew 5:33-37).*

In John and Paula Sanford's book, *Transformation of The Inner Man*, they define a vow this way: "An inner vow is a decision and resolve either to do or not to do a certain activity, event, or to have or not to have a certain attitude or relationship. It is a determination set by the mind and heart into all of one's being usually set early in life, and often forgotten."[2]

An example of a vow would be saying such things as, "I will never try again."(A decision which gives you a loser attitude; you just give up). Or, "I will never be like my father/mother" (A resolve regarding a relationship, which often results in you being exactly like the person you vowed you would never be like!); Or, "I never want children" (From someone who had a difficult upbringing or who gets disturbed by children's behavior; this is a decision which can even affect you physically); Or, "I will never allow myself to enjoy sex" (This is a resolve to not enjoy an activity or have an attitude towards sex as being anything but pleasurable, because of early abuse); Or, "I will never play baseball again;" (Because of something that happened to you, it could turn you into someone who avoids all sports); "I will never trust a woman again" (Maybe you were deeply hurt in a relationship).

In regards to inner vows Charles Kraft says, "People vow regularly to do things or not do things and that those vows that fall in line with Satan's purposes in our lives get empowered by him."[3] This makes perfect sense because Satan will take advantage of any opportunity to beat us down or destroy us. He will do anything he can do to keep us from reaching our potential in Christ.

Adolescence can be one of the toughest periods of our lives. During adolescence one's abilities, or lack thereof, can be cruelly attacked. If you are seen as stupid or too smart, you're going to be attacked. If you're too short or too tall, too fat or too skinny you will most likely be the object of somebody's ridicule. In junior high or high school, if you happen to be a little slower in developing physically you will be ridiculed. You're made fun of because of your body. If, during your growing years your father or some other significant person pushed you in athletics and you really didn't want to be in athletics it could have set you up for making an inner vow that would set the course of your life in a certain direction. The enemy is able to use such vows to establish a stronghold in a person.

CHARACTERISTICS OF AN INNER VOW

Let's review some of the characteristics of an inner vow. *An inner vow is a determination, and a directive sent into our inner being, which controls and blocks its energies and actions.* Inner vows are like railroad tracks and our mind is limited to run on the "track" set by the inner vow.

Inner vows resist change. In fact, quite often they refuse change. For instance, we normally mature out of childish ways but inner vows do not so easily surrender their hold on us. They resist the normal maturation process. Inner vows are usually made during childhood or adolescence and then are forgotten. As we grow we usually leave behind most of those things in our childish self such as awkwardness, brashness, immaturity, insensitivity towards others' feelings, etc.

Inner vows may not manifest immediately in behavior. They may rest, totally forgotten and dormant until triggered by the right persons or situations. Because we have forgotten them, we are unaware they exist or could have any effect. These vows need to be broken because their very nature is to prevent departure from them. Normally you cannot, unaided, uproot or change that vow. Only one who knows his authority in the Lord Jesus Christ can break a vow and reset the inner being to another way of acting.

Inner vows are sometimes indicated by compulsive behavior. They become unyielding obstructions in our nature, whose specific function is to hold us to feel, think, and act only as that vow has set the mold.

I've ministered to a number of people who only heard expressions of love or affirmation if they did what mommy or daddy wanted. For instance you may have grown up in a home where your mom said something like: "mommy loves you when you keep your room neat, or it makes mommy very upset when your room is messy." So you quickly figure out: if I keep my room neat mommy will love me. Later, this can translate into everything you do. It must be neat. The books and papers on your desk are all in neat order, bed made, clothes hung up in a proper order, etc. Nothing is out of order. I read an anonymous quote one time that said, "A neat desk is the sign of a sick mind."[4]

The strength of inner vows is enhanced when combined with a bitter root judgment, hidden resentment and/or fear. What is bitter root judgment? Here are some comments from John and Paula Sanford. "A bitter root judgment is a judgment held in one's heart in regard to the behavior or attitude of another. This unrepented judgment and its accompanying expectancy is like a seed sown that is later reaped in multiple returns. Bitter Root Judgments and expectancies are often unconscious, and have the power to influence, drive, and control perceptions, attitudes, and behavior until repented of and dealt with... Bitter root judgment also includes harboring ill will or making judgments toward parents or others with whom you have significant relationship. Judgments can turn inward as bitter roots and produce the same behavioral tendencies in yourself that you found hurtful and destructive from others! You come to expect things to be a certain way and consequently they always seem to turn out the way you expect them to."[5]

For instance, you may say: "I'll never be like my mother; she was always nagging on me and my dad." That judgment turns into bitterness and produces the same behavior in yourself that you found hurtful and destructive from your mother! You will probably be just like her in how you treat your spouse and children. Another judgment could be: "People will always let me down." "Men/Women will always hurt me." You have this bitter root in you and you expect things to be a certain way and they usually are! You come to distrust people, or close yourself off from people because you are sure that they always let you down or always hurt you. You might be living this way: you don't ever let people get very close and see the real you because they'll turn on you and hurt you. Have you been around people who never let you in; they always seem to have a wall up?

THERE ARE STEPS YOU CAN TAKE TO RESOLVE A BITTER ROOT JUDGMENT

Below is a summation of John and Paula Sanford's teaching about resolving bitter root judgments.

1. Ask the Holy Spirit to show you the original incident or pattern of incidents when you first made that bitter root judgment.

2. Forgive the person who hurt you or harmed another; release him or her from blame.

3. Repent and ask God to forgive you for holding that bitter root judgment. Remember that if you confess to God, he will forgive and cleanse you (I John 1:9). It is vital that you hate the bitter root judgment and the effects it has on your life. God desires us to actually hate what is evil (Romans 12:9b). Then ask Jesus for His blood to cleanse you from that bitter root judgment.

4. "In the name of Jesus break the power of that bitter root judgment and ask Jesus to apply His work on the cross between you and the reaping of that bitter root judgment." By doing this, you are saying that when Christ bore your

sins on the cross, that bitter root judgment was included, paid for, and made ineffective (1 Peter 2:24).

5. "Often personality structures and habit patterns are built around a single bitter root judgment and linger until separately dealt with. When you break a bitter root judgment, the war has been declared won; but do not become discouraged when minor battles and skirmishes emerge. Be faithful and trusting, allow God to help you through."[6]

Inner vows are as diverse as people are. Some are simple, like a boy who swears he will never sing (perhaps because of early embarrassment), only years later to discover a rich voice released. Some are complex, like a girl who refuses to put her head under water in swimming, but counsel discovers it has nothing to do with early swimming experiences and everything to do with a vow she made never to risk things beyond her control. People can make vows because of earlier experiences like, "I will never wear hand-me-downs", or "I will never allow my personal space to be invaded."

Many inner vows have to do with ambitions, or rebellions against them. "'I'll never fail again," "I'll be the best ever," or "I'll never try again." These kinds of things can cause people to become driven, or to just give up. Some of the most destructive are those concerning personal relationships. Children can make powerful determinations against parents that will later work to destroy their own marital relationships.

Some inner vows set a person upon illogical courses that lead to breakdowns or explosions. "I'll never let my temper go again; see what resulted when I did." Such a person thereafter may store up repressed angers until, finally, a merest spark sets off a holocaust. Have you ever been around someone who suddenly explodes over something that is so insignificant? I mean, they really go ballistic and everyone is shocked at what is going on. The cause could very well go back to a vow to not ever lose your temper.

I'm not saying it's okay to lose your temper, but we can't just keep stuffing things because at some point we are going to explode.

We need healthy ways to deal with anger. If you have made an inner vow to never get angry, you will not be able to deal with your anger but you will just keep stuffing it until you fly into a rage.

THE VOWS WE MAKE

We may make many vows as adults, but these lack the controlling power of vows made in those childhood formative years, which set the shape of our character. It is possible for the entire structure of a personality to be built around one inner vow. Such as, "I'll never trust people again." That can shape your whole personality, your whole life! You don't trust anybody and it consequently determines how you react and respond to people. It's important to know that inner vows are usually made before teen years, and then forgotten, having more power by their subliminal and invisible nature.

John and Paula Sandford tell of a woman who came to them who could not bear a male child. She had become pregnant several times and had miscarried boys about the third or fourth month. As they questioned her and prayed they learned that when she was growing up her brother took his teasing beyond the usual sibling rivalry. He was vicious, continually embarrassing her and physically hurting her. She remembered at about nine or ten, walking beside a river, picking up stones, hurling them; into the water, crying out, "I'll never carry a boy child." That was an inner vow. "Though the conscious mind had long forgotten, the inner being had not. Though she now wanted to give birth to a male child, the earlier programming (the inner vow), was still intact and functioning." I cannot explain logically how something said into our inner being affects the physiological functions of our physical being but time and again we have prayed for people regarding inner vows they made and have seen significant change. In this particular case they reported that she was able after the vow was broken to bear a beautiful, healthy male child.[7]

Not all inner vows are negative vows. Some may seem to us to be very good vows. Let's say we got into an argument with someone and were so upset or embarrassed over it that we make a vow never to argue again. We may respond by saying; "I will never confront anyone again; I will always be a peacemaker." What this can do is prevent us from even entering into a healthy discussion on issues that we may feel strongly about but don't want to risk the consequences of a confrontation. Or we could make an inner vow that may cause us to be gentle, when the Lord would call us to be stern.

Inner vows need to be broken, because they force us to try to rely on the power of our flesh to be good or righteous, or protected, or free from conflict.

BREAKING INNER VOWS

Breaking these vows requires recognition, repentance, authority and perseverance.

Recognition: We profit best by remembering that we made an inner vow, and that we can accomplish freedom by faith, recognizing that an unseen vow might be there, as yet invisible and undefeated. Ask the Holy Spirit to help you remember any inner vows you may have made.

Repentance: We need to repent of the sinful reactions that caused us to make the vow in the first place - for example, hate, resentment, vengeance, etc.

Authority: Authority can break inner vows. As believers we have available to us access to the same authority with which Jesus functioned. As you learn who you are in Christ you will begin to understand what this authority is. Once you begin to understand the authority you have, then you will begin to learn how to use it.

Perseverance: Perseverance in prayer is needed as you struggle to overcome long practiced and deeply ingrained habits. Prayerful persistence can break the hold these vows have over you.

STUBBORN PRACTICES

How do we find inner vows? Most often we identify them by observation and asking the Holy Spirit to reveal them. Look for inner vows behind stubborn practices in your old nature. Compulsive behavior may indicate inner vows at their root. Where inner vows do lie at the root, seldom are they the sole factor. They work in tandem with bitter roots, hidden resentments and fears, etc. The crucial factor concerning inner vows is that if they are at the root, they are often the key to healing and freedom.

Be aware of the complexity of the personality structure built around an inner vow. Even after they are broken, the structures often remain, and must be dealt with. For example, let's say you find it hard to trust women or men, and for thirty or forty years you've had to deal with that. All of a sudden you find out that you made a vow as a twelve year old to never trust women or never trust men. Your entire personality is built around that vow. You break the vow, and then you've still got to learn how to trust. You have to restore how you see yourself.

When you're around some people they come across to you as winners. Others come across to you as losers. It's as if they project "I'm a loser, I know I'm a loser, I know you're going to reject me, I'm not even going to try to do anything to make you like me." Your attitude about what you are, or who you are, projects to other people. There's something about our spirit that either connects or doesn't connect with some people. Spiritually you can read people and much of the time what you are reading may be a vow they made against themselves.

STEPS TO BREAK AN INNER VOW

1. Begin with a hatred of your inner vow and its effects. You must start with a strong desire to break that inner vow.

2. Repent and confess your inner vow before the Lord. Forgive anyone who hurt you, then ask God to forgive you for making the vow and cleanse you with the blood of Jesus.

3. In the name of Jesus break the inner vow and its influence in your life. It is essential that you have personal faith in the power and will of the Lord to act in your behalf. As you pray, express this breaking in several ways, so your entire being can take hold of your new freedom.

Here is an example of what you can pray to break a vow.

"I break this inner vow of_____in Jesus name, and in Jesus name I am released from bondage to freedom. Thank you Jesus, for freeing me from this vow, and restoring me to health."

ANCESTRAL VOWS

There are two kinds of negative vows that need to be broken; those inner vows we make as we just described, and ancestral vows that are passed down to us.

Our ancestors made vows that are passed from generation to generation. The obvious question is, "How can I be responsible for what my ancestors did and how can I do anything about it?" Understand this, we are covered in the blood of Jesus Christ. He can protect us from even the things that we don't know about. Paul writes in Romans about the law and how before the law came you didn't know about sin (Romans 3:19). After the law came and made you aware of sin (Romans 5:13), the grace of Jesus Christ came and covered over the law, covered over the sin (Romans 7:4-6). So the grace of Christ is able to deal with sins, including ancestral vows, that we haven't known about before.

As we begin to learn about vows we can ask the Lord to reveal to us vows that were made by our ancestors.

"Dr. Charles Kraft tells the story of a colleague who dealt with the descendant of a woman who had made an openly evil vow. She had actually written a letter to Satan, vowing to give him her firstborn son, and every firstborn son thereafter of her descendants, if he would make her rich and famous. She became rich and famous, but her descendant, a firstborn son, was in deep trouble. They were eventually able to break this vow off of the child and bring about some significant change.[8]

This is what we would clearly call an ancestral vow. It was passed down from a mother to her children. Ancestors can be involved in witchcraft, Satan worship, and different practices of the occult. The vows that they make can be passed from generation to generation.

They can involve themselves in rituals and bring curses on a family that are passed down generationally.

It's not uncommon for me to deal with people whose relatives were involved in witchcraft or the occult, generations back and they are still dealing with its effects.

To break ancestral vows we claim authority in the name of Jesus to break their power. Often that is effective and all that needs to be done. If you need to know exactly what the vow is the Lord will reveal that to you. You can pray something like the following to break ancestral vows:

> *"In the name of Jesus, I take authority over all vows in my father's and mother's lines and cancel any power given to the enemy, and break his power through vows that may have been made by any of my ancestors in my father's or mother's line."*[9]

AUTHORITY OVER THE PAST

There may be some question in your mind regarding how we can do this when someone else made the vow. One of the areas covered by our authority in Christ is not obvious to many. It is a right we have received to cancel any claims the enemy may be able to make on us due to events and agreements of the past. In this case we are talking about some of the rights the enemy has over people through the generational bloodline. Believers have the authority to cancel those rights.

The place to start is with the recognition that God has planned and chosen each of us from before the creation of the world. *For He chose us in Him before the creation of the world to be holy and blameless in His sight* (Ephesians.1: 4). We can then assume that He was aware of each pair of our ancestors and the transmission of both genetic and spiritual influences down through the generations.

According to Psalm 139:13, He formed and framed us in our mother's womb so we would come out just right. However, we live in an evil and wicked world where we are influenced by numerous things. The enemy has had ample opportunity through this process to influence and often to intrude on our ancestry by way of demonization.

HOW DOES THE ENEMY DO THIS?

Through choices our ancestors have made, doors can often be opened into our bloodlines, permitting the enemy to produce damage and insert his agents that will be inherited from generation to generation, such as their involvement in witchcraft or the example I gave earlier regarding the woman who dedicated her firstborn to Satan.

To help free you from any such bondages, it is important to take authority over them and cancel all rights the enemy may have gained not only through vows, but to also take authority over curses, dedications, sin and trauma. It is important for us, whether by ourselves or with the help of another, to take authority over these issues in our ancestry in such a way as to cancel any rights the enemy may have gained in our lives deriving from the past.

In regards to breaking these ancestral vows, any Christian who understands their authority in Christ can break a vow. One who does not truly know the Lord nor believe his own authority in the Lord cannot say it as a magic ritual. An example is in Acts 19:13-16. The Seven sons of Sceva discovered when they tried to apply the name of Jesus in an unbelieving manner, the enemy did not recognize their power.

To break the power of ancestral vows we claim authority in the name of Jesus. This often is effective unless the power of Satan through a given vow is so great that we must discover what the vow was and break it quite specifically.

If you come up against a vow that is so strong that you feel you do not have the authority or power to break it I recommend you find some ministry resources that can help walk you through freedom from these vows. One such resource would be Wholeness Ministries in Bakersfield California, whose contact information is available at the back of this book. Another excellent resource is Dr. Charles Kraft with Hearts Set Free in Pasadena, California.

Vows, whether made by us, or by an ancestor, can become as spiritually damaging to our growth as Christians as any of the other kinds of baggage we have talked about so far. But Jesus Christ is present to enable us to break them and leave them, once and for all.

HARMFUL WORDS, HARMFUL CONNECTIONS

The Power of Curses and Soul Ties

> *They fully intend to topple him from his lofty place; they take delight in lies. With their mouths they bless, but in their hearts they curse (Psalm 62:4).*

In my travels in the United States and internationally I have discovered that many in the church today do not know about curses and soul ties. For much of my life I did not have a clue that these existed or, how to get free from them. In addition to not knowing about curses and soul ties we do not fully understand the authority we have in Jesus Christ to break free from them. I want to explore specifically what these are, how they affect us, and the power and authority we have to break free from their influence in our lives. Let's begin with curses.

HARMFUL WORDS

To curse is to invoke, speak, or pronounce evil upon oneself or upon others. Curses come to a person in a variety of ways and primarily involve the spoken word, although thoughts play a definitive role.

TWO TYPES OF CURSES

"**Informal cursing** can happen when making such statements as "You'll never amount to anything." It can be swearing or cursing such as "You good for nothing (blank-blank)," "You fool, you idiot!", "You are so stupid!" These are curses especially if someone in authority speaks these words over you. When this happens the words can be empowered by the enemy to work against you. These words can slice into a child or adult like a knife and remain for a lifetime until Jesus replaces the lie with the truth of who you really are. These negative judgments or curses can destroy a child's self-esteem. They bring about shame, a feeling of basic worthlessness. The curse could even go back to pre-birth especially if the pregnancy was not wanted or if the parents wanted a child of the opposite sex. Either parent may put a curse on the child by saying, "I wish I/you weren't pregnant," or "I hope there will be a miscarriage."

Formal Cursing involves the performance of a ritual, in which words are spoken and sometimes an image or statue of the person being cursed is used, in order to invoke satanic power against that person. This is typically done by people heavily involved in the occult who want to send a curse against you."[1]

FIVE WAYS WE CAN COME UNDER A CURSE

Speaking a curse on yourself. This may happen through careless or angry words, such as "I wish I were dead", "I hate myself", "I'll never be successful." Though we may say these things in anger, often we truly believe them. That belief begins to affect how we feel about ourselves and that begins to influence how we act. The most frequent target of self-curses seems to be our bodies, often during adolescence. Because of shame or insecurity we curse some part of ourselves; maybe our face, breasts, legs, sex organs, or some other parts that we do not feel are adequate. As our bodies develop, we may perceive ourselves to be the object of critical words or looks from peers, especially if the speed of our development differs from that of others. It's not unusual to minister to men who have cursed themselves, and whose struggle with shame is intense due to the taunts of their peers in high school locker rooms and gym classes. Our bodies all develop at different rates and it can be tough if you are a little slow in reaching puberty when all the guys around you are way ahead of where you are in your development. Shame and insecurity is also a frequent problem in women. It could happen either because of dissatisfaction with how they developed or because of early childhood abuse. Many have cursed themselves or part of themselves, because they do not feel that they measure up to the kind of body the media portrays that they must have."[2]

Cursing your birth or gender. Another form of self-cursing is that we should not have been born, or that we should have been of the opposite sex. Because of circumstances surrounding our conception or trauma experienced in early childhood many have said: "I didn't deserve to be born, I shouldn't be here, I wish I were dead because I've just caused great trouble for my mom." "I know my dad really wanted a boy and I hate my body because I'm a girl."[3]

In his book, *I Give You Authority*, Dr. Charles Kraft, tells the story of a woman who was the fourth daughter in a Chinese family. She came to him because she had cancer in several parts of her body. In the course of the conversation he asked her if she had ever wished she were a boy. "Every second of my life!" she replied. Then she admitted to having cursed her body thousands of times. Through prayer he helped her renounce the curses and later received a letter from her that she was well."[4]

Scripture speaks about uttering curses: *Cursed be the day I was born! May the day my mother bore me not be blessed!* (Jeremiah 20:14),

How do we break curses that we have spoken against ourselves? It begins with asking God's forgiveness and then in the name of Jesus renouncing the curse and all its power in your life.

Others speaking a curse against you. We have ministered to people who have come out of such religious backgrounds as Buddhism or Hinduism. When an individual from one of these backgrounds becomes a Christian it is not uncommon for the family to formally curse them. We prayed for a lady from Taiwan who was having nightmares almost daily and finding it extremely difficult to sleep. As we prayed for her I stopped at one point and said, "I keep seeing this dragon. Does that mean anything to you?" She began to tell me about these silk pajamas her mother had sent her from Taiwan that had this beautiful dragon embroidered on the front. As she talked it became clear that the pajamas were the problem. Her family is Buddhist. When she became a Christian her mother and father were very angry and rejected her. What the Lord revealed to us was that her mother had cursed these pajamas in a ceremony and sent them to her daughter because of her rejection of their religion. I told her to destroy the pajamas and she would be able to sleep without the horrible nightmares. We prayed to rebuke the curses. Then she went home and destroyed the pajamas. When she came back the next week, her report was that she was able to sleep through the night without any nightmares.

It is not unusual for curses to be sent against pastors, teachers or other leaders involved in Christian ministry. Missionaries overseas as well as Christian workers in the United States seem to be special targets of cursing. In the area where we live there are satanic covens that regularly send out curses against Christians. Don't be naïve, we are in warfare and the enemy hates us and will do anything to stop or destroy us.

A number of years ago I woke up at 2:45am two nights in a row. I felt something evil in the room but just ignored it and went back to sleep. It bothered me but I really didn't know what it was or why it was there. A couple of days later in a conversation with Francis MacNutt, he told me that it is very common for those involved in witchcraft and satanic rituals to send out curses against Christians between the hours of Midnight and 3:00am. Just as we Christians pray to God and send our prayers and blessings to others, so do those involved in witchcraft and Satan worship. The difference is that they are sending out curses to their enemies. Guess who their enemies are? So the next night when I awoke with this evil presence in the room I said, "In the name of Jesus I command you to go back to where you came from and never return again." From then on I slept great! There was no more waking up at 2:45am.

These scriptures speak about others cursing you.

> *When Noah woke up from his drunken stupor, he learned what Ham, his youngest had done. Then he cursed the descendents of Canaan, the son of Ham; "A curse on the Canaanites! May they be the lowest of servants to the descendants of Shem and Japheth." (Genesis 9:24-25, NLT)*

> *Do not blaspheme God or curse anyone who rules over you (Exodus 22:28, NLT).*

...bless those who curse you, pray for those who mistreat you (Luke 6:28).

Numbers 22 and 23 show how seriously God takes curses. He would not allow Balaam to curse the Israelites.

How do we break a formal or informal curse against us? Begin by asking the Lord to reveal to you any curses spoken against you. Then forgive the person who spoke evil against you, and bless them. Last, in the name of Jesus renounce the curse, refuse its hold on you, and break its power.

Curses through generational sin. There are activities our ancestors may have been involved in that can affect us even if we do not know about them. If anyone in our family line has made vows giving the enemy rights, or put curses on themselves or the family, or made dedications through occult involvement, or granted power to Satan through sinful practices, we will be affected. But, we have the authority to renounce those agreements made by our ancestors and the effects of the curses.

One summer I was at a weeklong retreat in Green Lake, Wisconsin. During the course of the week a pastor and his wife came to me asking for prayer for their son who was about seven years old. They told me that his behavior was out of control and they were at their wits end on what they could do to cope with the effect he was having on their entire family. They had tried everything they knew to discipline this child but nothing worked. When they tried to pray for him he would become very agitated. I agreed to go over to their cabin after they put their son to bed and pray for him while he was sleeping. When I arrived they took me into the room where he was sleeping and I knelt beside the bed, placed my hand on him and began to pray. I didn't know what to pray so I began to ask the Lord to guide me. As I was praying and listening to the Lord I heard the words American Indian. I thought that was curious because neither Isaac nor his parents looked as if they had any American Indian heritage. When I asked the mother she told me that her mother was full blood Cherokee. Knowing that in their culture there is a lot of worship of spirits I prayed that if anything was passed down through the generational line that was not from God that it would leave. As I prayed, Isaac immediately began to fidget and flop around the bed, obviously very agitated. This went on for a few seconds and then he suddenly became completely still. During this entire prayer he never woke up. After I finished praying I left and went back to where I was staying and went to sleep.

The next morning the father and mother came running up to me with these huge grins telling me that when their son awoke this morning he was a different child. Calm, nice and obedient were some of the words they used to describe him. As the days passed it was obvious to everyone who knew him that his behavior had changed completely. They said, "We don't know where our former son went but we like this new one much better!" Obviously there was something in the generational line that was affecting him. Even though I didn't specifically know what the spirit was, to pray the way I did was sufficient to cut off the power and influence of what was causing the rebellion and the rages that he would fly into over the smallest things. Many years later we have observed that this old son never returned. In fact, he went on to become involved in significant work with missions.

These scriptures speak to generational curses:

> *"Do not make idols of any kind, whether in the shape of birds or animals or fish. You must never worship or bow down to them, for I, the Lord your God, am a jealous God who will not share your affection with any other god! I do not leave unpunished the sins of those who hate me, but I punish the children for the sins of their parents to the third and fourth generations" (Exodus 20:4-6, NLT)*

> *The Lord is slow to anger and rich in unfailing love, forgiving every kind of sin and rebellion. Even so he does not leave sin unpunished, but he punishes the children for the sins of their parents to the third and fourth generation (Numbers 14:18 NLT)*

> *Remember that Christ's work on the cross is sufficient to cover all our sins, including generational sins. Yet it was our weaknesses he carried; it was our sorrows that weighed him down. And we thought his troubles were a punishment from God for his own sins! But he was wounded and crushed for our sins. He was beaten that we might have peace. He was whipped, and we were healed! All of us have strayed away like sheep. We have left God's paths to follow our own. Yet the Lord laid on him the guilt and sins of us all (Isaiah 53: 4-6, NLT).*

But, like salvation, healing, and forgiveness, freedom from the curse of generational sin must be appropriated. Generational, or inherited sin does not cause me to sin, but it creates a weakness for that particular sin to reoccur - much like the physical realm where a propensity for certain diseases can be inherited. The consequences of this type of sin tend to pass down from generation to generation. We have observed in some the weakness for drugs or alcohol that are evident in past generations.

How do we break generational curses? Pray and ask God to help you identify the generational sin either by its action, such as idolatry, or its effects, such as broken relationships. Pray and take responsibility for the sins of the past generations and ask for the blood of Christ to cleanse you. Renounce the sin in the name of Jesus and cut off any linkage between you and previous generations in that sin, and declare that curse broken.

Curses through occult involvement. This can be occult involvement by past generations or by you personally. These vows, dedications and curses also need to be renounced. Many people who come for prayer ministry have participated in occult activities. Much of this involvement came innocently through playing with Ouija boards or games like Dungeons and Dragons. Some came from being involved in organizations like Scientology, Freemasonry, Christian Science or Mormonism. The rights given the enemy through such involvement must be renounced.

A mother called me to come over to her home and pray through her son's room. As I was in his room praying with him

Before You Get Here

I felt tremendous evil and noticed that on his bookshelves were several books having to do with occult games. He told me he was quite heavily involved in playing Dungeons and Dragons and had what they call the "Master Book."

I said to him, "You should get rid of those books by burning them." He wasn't ready to do that yet but said he would think and pray about it. Later that night he called me, quite frightened and related this story. "I felt the Lord told me to destroy the books, so I went down to our fireplace and threw them into the flames. When I did that with the Master Book these strange noises began to come from the fireplace, the flames turned blue and yellow and green then all at once the book exploded and it was over. Scared the snot out of me, Mike - what was that?" Fortunately I was able to tell him and help get rid of a great deal of other stuff he was involved in. That then brought to him freedom from those evil influences.

These scriptures speak regarding occult involvement:

> *You must worship no other Gods, but only the Lord, for he is a God who is passionate about his relationship with you. Do not make treaties of any kind with the people living in the land. They are spiritual prostitutes, committing adultery against me by sacrificing to their gods. If you make peace with them, they will invite you to go with them to worship their gods, and you are likely to do it (Exodus 34:14-15, NLT).*

> *If any among the people are unfaithful by consulting and following mediums or psychics, I will turn against them and cut them off from the community (Leviticus 20:6, NLT).*

Remember that God clearly commands us to stay clear of occult involvement. When we do not, we come under a curse, and a spiritual gloom of darkness falls on us until we repent and are cleansed by the blood of Jesus.

How do we break curses because of occult involvement? First you must confess and repent of your specific occult involvement. Then in the name of Jesus renounce that practice, pray to break off its consequences and ask for the cleansing of Jesus' blood. You must then destroy any books or paraphernalia connected with that occult practice.

Curses through disobedience. If you walk in continual disobedience to God in any particular area, you run the risk of opening yourself up to bondage to a curse. Some of the sins of disobedience are rebellion, idolatry or immorality. If you continually look at pornography you are opening yourself up to those pictures and images that become a curse in your thought life. You keep trying to break free from the thoughts but you are unable to because of disobedience. If you are involved in immoral behavior, it is a curse on your life!

These scriptures speak specifically to disobedience:

> *But if you refuse to listen to the Lord your God and do not obey all the commands and laws I am giving you today, all these curses will come and overwhelm you (Deuteronomy 28:15, NLT).*
>
> *Rebellion is as bad as the sin of witchcraft, and stubbornness is as bad as worshiping idols. So because you have rejected the word of the Lord, he has rejected you from being king (1 Samuel 15:23, NLT).*

Disobedience is a transgression of God's covenant and brings a curse that includes the wrath of God. Only by confession and forgiveness through Christ can we be restored, for Christ is the final and perfect answer to the broken fellowship brought about by disobeying.

How do we break curses due to disobedience? As you pray, confess and repent of your disobedience, ask Jesus to cleanse you and break any curses in your life and determine to walk in obedience to God. Doing so will release the baggage of sin and possible curses that Satan wants to keep piling on you.

HARMFUL CONECTIONS - SPIRITUAL AND PSYCHOLOGICAL SOUL TIES

Soul ties are bonds empowered by Satan that come about in a variety of ways and usually involve sex, close friendship or dominating relationships.

One of the easiest soul ties to recognize is an adult man who is still overly dependent on his mother. He has never quite cut the "apron strings." Psychological ties normally change as a person matures. Typically we grow out of being dominated by our parents. If this change doesn't occur, chances are that an unhealthy spiritual tie has formed as well. That tie needs to be severed through prayer. A soul tie can be formed when we are bonded to people who dominate us, or with whom we have an unnatural or super-intense friendship or dependent relationship.

A pastor who is very dominating can produce a church that has so many demands on people, it is like a cult. There may be so many strict rules and regulations that before members can make any major decision, they must ask the leader's permission. This can result in psychological soul ties that need to be severed through prayer.

There are many kinds of relationships, especially sexual ones that may crowd out a person's rightful independence. These need to be cut loose through prayer. Sexual relationships bond people spiritually. This is why Paul put sexual sin in a special category because unlike other sins, sexual sin works within and against the body, which is God's Temple.

> *Do you not know that your bodies are members of Christ himself? Shall I then take the members of Christ and unite them with a prostitute? Never! Do you not know that he who unites himself with a prostitute is one with her in body? For it is said, "The two will become one flesh." But he who unites himself with the Lord is one with him in spirit. Flee from sexual immorality. All other sins a man commits are outside his body, but he who sins sexually sins against his own body. Do you not know that your body is a temple of the Holy Spirit, who is in you, whom you have received from God? You are not your own; you were bought at a price. Therefore honor God with your body (1 Corinthians 6:15-20.*

THE GRAVITY OF SEXUAL SIN

Sexual intimacy bonds people to each other. Something more takes place than the mere joining of two bodies; there is a bonding that takes place spiritually and relationally. Paul does not say exactly what kind of union takes place when a man becomes one flesh with a prostitute, but he seems to teach that something takes place in the spiritual realm.

In Francis MacNutt's book, *Deliverance From Evil Spirits*, he quotes Tommy Tyson as saying; "Whenever anyone engages in a full sexual relationship, a permanent bond is set up that remains until it is broken, not by the couple's breaking up, but by something like a prayer for deliverance. If a man has had a sexual relationship with six women before he marries, he brings six people besides himself into the marriage bed and spiritual confusion is brought into that marriage from the beginning."[5] In our work we have ministered to adults who have had so many sexual partners that they can't remember them all.

People bonded by sex to persons other than their marriage partners carry a major source of satanic interference in their lives. In their book, *The Transformation of the Inner Man*, John and Paula Sanford write, "Any complete sexual act, whether fornication, adultery, homosexuality or some other aberration, unites a person's spirit with the other. God has so built us in our spirits that whatever woman a man enters, their spirits are united to each other from that moment on. Each person's spirit seeks, from the moment of union, to find, fulfill, nurture, and cherish the one who entered into that union with him/her... Once a wrong union has been entered, our spirit still remembers that union and seeks to fulfill the other. We are tied spiritually to that other individual...If there have been many immoral unions with many partners, our spirit becomes like an overloaded transformer, trying to send its current in too many directions."[6]

There is within our culture today a very casual attitude toward sex. It is not unusual for teens to engage in various forms of sexual activity. In ministry we often encounter people who had sexual experiences as young teens of thirteen or fourteen. This experience, which may have happened only once, sets them up for a struggle that is very difficult to overcome because of the sexual soul tie that was formed but never dealt with.

During adolescence young boys are especially vulnerable to this because there is often sexual experimentation where sexual activities are engaged in with other boys. Where there is sexual intercourse or oral sex there is a soul tie formed.

CANCELING SOUL TIES

Dr. Charles Kraft writes, "To deal with adultery, incest, rape, homosexual encounters, or any other extra-marital relations we first make sure the person has confessed to God any sin involved and received his forgiveness. If it was adultery or homosexuality, the whole thing needs to be confessed as sin. Rape or incest, however, since they are not the fault of the victim, are not confessed as sin. But there may be areas of anger, bitterness, unforgiveness, and the like that need to be confessed to God as sin before the person can be helped.

Once the sin has been dealt with, we ask the person to go back to the affair(s) under the guidance of the Holy Spirit, picturing the person and, if necessary, forgiving that person for his or her part in the relationship. The person then is guided to release/cut in the name of Jesus, all soul ties to all persons he/she has had sex with, excluding the current marriage partner.

The way to break these sexual bonds or soul ties is to use our authority that we have as believers to first renounce the relationship and then claim the freedom Jesus gives us when we break such enemy power. Usually it is enough for you to state something like:

> "I renounce the sexual bonding and cut the soul tie I have with <u>(name)</u> in Jesus' name, and break the power Satan has gained over me through this relationship."

Praying for someone to be set free from undue physical, psychological or spiritual bondage is relatively easy. Some examples of prayer would be:

> "In the name of Jesus Christ, I set you free from any physical, psychological or spiritual bond that remains within you, caused by your past sexual relationship."

Or, you can have them pray:

> "I renounce the sexual bonding or soul tie I have with (_____) in Jesus' name, and break the power Satan has gained over me through this relationship."

Breaking the soul ties and their power is easier than breaking the habits that were formed. Once the power is broken, the person needs to work hard at establishing new habits."[7]

Once you become aware of curses and soul-ties, you can begin to see the effect they can have on your life. Part of what I have tried to do is help you understand what these are. More importantly is that you have the power and authority through the Holy Spirit to break the power of these bondages over your life. You can be set free from curses spoken against you, words you've spoken against yourself, and psychological, spiritual soul ties. There truly is freedom in Jesus Christ!

LET YOURSELF BE LOVED BY GOD

Another kind of baggage that needs to be dropped is a serious misunderstanding of, and resistance to, the intense love that God has for each of us.

Do you ever wonder why God would even bother with us? On a typical day most of us are entangled in a hundred thoughts and activities that have nothing to do with God. We do things that are in our best interest with little thought about how God might feel about what we are doing. But He is closer than our breath or heartbeat. Scripture tells us that He created us, freed us, saved us, and seeks us. He continually beckons, and He is there to comfort us. He makes himself available to us and yet He gives us the freedom to make our own choices independent of Him. We may receive what He has to offer or not. The choice is ours.

Again, I ask why God would even bother with us. In thinking about this question and exploring Scripture and the writings of others as well as considering my own experience, the conclusion for me was simple. The answer is love. What else would motivate Him to create us with a free will, then release us to make choices knowing that someday He would have to send His son Jesus to die for us? What makes Him bother with us? I believe it is LOVE!

> *I have loved you with an everlasting love; I have drawn you with loving-kindness* (Jeremiah 31:3).

HOW DEEP IS THIS LOVE?

I want you to try and grasp the depth of God's love. When we do this we will be drawn to want to respond to Him. *And may you have the power to understand, as all God's people should, how wide, how long, how high, and how deep his love really is* (Ephesians 3:18).

Furthermore it is important to remember this:

> *And I am convinced that nothing can ever separate us from his love. Death can't, and life can't. The angels can't, and the demons can't. Our fears for today, our worries about tomorrow, and even the powers of hell can't keep God's love away. Whether we are high above the sky or in the deepest ocean, nothing in all creation will ever be able to separate us from the love of God that is revealed in Christ Jesus our Lord* (Romans 8:38-39, TLB).

But I think for many of us it is difficult to understand and experience the deep, intensely personal love of God, this Agape love which is unconditional. Think about how bizarre it is that you can be loved simply as you are with all your sins and faults. This love is irrational to a thinking person. You don't need to do anything, give anything or prove yourself worthy in any way. You are loved simply because you are.

One of my favorite authors, A.W. Tozer, wrote, "It is a strange and beautiful eccentricity of the free God that he has allowed his heart to be emotionally identified with men. Self-sufficient as he is, he wants our love and will not be satisfied till he gets it. Free as he is, he has let his heart be bound to us forever."[1]

Can you grasp that? God allows himself to be affected by our love. Whether we give it or withhold it, it is important to Him and it has an emotional affect on Him. Why would God do this? LOVE! In the first book of the Bible, Genesis 1, it says: *In the beginning God created,* and *Let us make man in our image...* why? LOVE! Because God is love and love requires a response. He created us and put within us the capacity to respond.

In the last book of the Bible we read, *Behold, I stand at the door and knock* (Revelation 3:20). Why? LOVE! Imagine if you can, from Genesis to Revelation, we have recorded thousands of years of God's history with man, which have one long tale of rebellion, disobedience and rejection of God by man. And yet He doesn't change! God is wrapped up in mankind. He created us for his glory, for fellowship with him, and for his pleasure. He has been reaching out for personal involvement with us from the beginning as recorded in Genesis, and he is still reaching out.

You may be thinking, yes I know that God loves all of mankind but does He love me as an individual? Is His love personal?

The cross gives us the greatest sense of personal love. Christ did not die simply for mankind in general, but as Paul wrote: *Christ loved me and gave himself for me* (Galatians 2:20). Further we read in John that *God so loved the world that he gave his one and only Son, that whoever believes in him shall not perish but have eternal life (John 3:16)*. He calls each of us individually, Christ died for you personally and for me personally. He is my Savior, I am His child.

LET YOURSELF BE LOVED BY GOD

Begin with the appreciation and realization of the concrete meaning of God's love for you, just as you are and not as you should be. His love is not based on your performance. Being still and waiting is not an activity of mind but a passive mode of receiving. Like slipping into a tub of hot water, let God's love seep in, saturate, and permeate every part of your being.

Henri Nouwen expressed God's loving words to us this way: "I am your God, you are my child. How can you ever doubt that I will embrace you again, hold you against my breast, kiss you, and let my hands run through your hair? I am a God of mercy and compassion, of tenderness and care. I so much want you to be close to me. I know all your thoughts. I hear all your words. I see all of your actions. And I love you. Do not judge yourself. Do not condemn yourself. Do not reject yourself. Let my love touch the most hidden corners of your heart and reveal to you your beauty, a beauty that you have lost sight of. Come, let me wipe away your tears, and let my mouth come close to your ear and say to you, 'I love you, I love you, I love you."[2]

WHY NOT?

If much of your journey with God consists of doing things for Him, then you are missing the best part of the journey. God does not want your doing as much as He wants you. If you are tired of seeking approval in superficial relationships or working to live up to someone else's expectations, then get alone with God and just hang out with Him. If you can stop your pretense and striving for approval long enough to sit quietly with God, there you will find that you are significant, accepted and loved. Regardless of your personal circumstances, your weaknesses and even your sins, God wants to be with you.

He will not love you any more or any less because of what you do or do not do. He will not love you any more tomorrow than He loves you today. He loves you as much as He will ever love you.

He *wants* to be with you. His heart longs for you! Even more than that, He created you so that He could be with you. That is your purpose for being! We are His chosen, set apart, loved ones - and nothing we do can change that.

As you pursue a closer walk with the Lord, as you pursue a life of spending more time with Him, I encourage you to grasp the reality of God and remember who He is. Keep in mind that the King of Kings, the Lord of Lords, our Creator and the Creator of the universe is offering us the opportunity to spend as much time *as we want* with Him. We can worship Him, talk to Him, listen to Him and let Him love us. That should cause us to stand amazed. So why not enjoy the journey? Why not allow yourself permission to just be with Him? Why not claim your place at His side?

The baggage we carry around of low self worth and feelings of inadequacy keep us from God's love. The idea that we must constantly do something to earn his love or do something that will keep Him happy is not from God. It is a trick of the enemy and must be dealt with in order for us to move to a place where we cannot only begin to understand God's love for us but also let ourselves be loved by God.

HOW CAN THIS BE?

I find it difficult to fully grasp how God could love me so completely and unconditionally. When I am honest enough to be transparent with Him and myself, and accept how ugly and sinful I am without Him, I stand amazed that He wants to be with me.

We should be completely blown away that He loves us and forgives us unconditionally. When you think back over your life and what you have done, when you honestly examine yourself and what you think or say or do, do you not stand amazed that He is always there, that He will never leave you or forsake you?

As I continue this journey with God, I am beginning to grasp with my simple mind that what God is revealing about Himself is absolutely staggering! Pause and think about this for a moment. The God of the universe is urging, inviting and persuading us to spend time with Him. He is willing to reveal Himself to us and transform and conform us to the image of Jesus Christ. He wants to have relationship with us. Let's not allow ourselves to be distracted by a new layer of religious knowledge, a new doctrine or a new spiritual insight. Let's seek to simply grasp the reality of God's love!

I read somewhere that love was defined as, "A strong personal attachment and ardent affection which includes three things: First, sympathetic understanding, second, good will and benevolent kind action, and third, delight and pleasure in the loved one."[3] It's obvious that God's love for us includes all of these.

We experience love in numerous ways in our life. Perhaps you can remember that "first love" which would occasionally cause you to act as if you were not in a sane state of mind. Love can do that to you. I suspect you can remember doing something when you were head over heels in love, that when you look back on that now you may wonder, what was I thinking! As we grow in love we move into a deeper level that goes far beyond those warm fuzzy feelings to something that may be difficult to put into words. This is a natural progression of love which most of us experience in various ways.

THIS MUCH

The reality of this love came to me during a healing conference I attended at the Anaheim Vineyard in California in the late 1980s. John Wimber had invited all the pastors to come forward for prayer. We gathered up near the stage and as John prayed I began with deep sobs to sink to my knees. I do not know how long I remained there on my knees, but when I stood up I was flooded with the most incredible warmth of God's love I had ever felt. As

I stood there with my eyes closed and my hands raised I asked, "God, how much do you love me?" Immediately I saw in my mind a picture of two hands with the palms open, with deep wounds in them, coming down through the clouds. The moment I realized whose hands they were I felt something touch my open palms and I heard God say, "This much." I was overwhelmed with the depth of God's love for me and wept like a little child, sobbing with joy, unashamed and completely oblivious to those around me. Later as I composed myself I realized what a profound moment that was for me. What an amazing way for God to let me know how much I was loved.

Scripture declares, *How great is the love the Father has lavished on us* (1 John 3:1). To *lavish* means "to give or bestow in abundance." Have you ever allowed God the Father to love you in this way? Have you allowed Him to so totally pour His love over you that you are overwhelmed and cannot even stand?

In the game of tennis "Love" is a score of zero. And that's how it is for many of us in the game of life, a score of zero. We've never known the love that we can receive from God, and how drastically different it is from the love this world offers. To try and understand the love that God has for us is so far beyond our grasp that it can be incomprehensible.

DOES HE UNDERSTAND?

What is His love like? He wants us near him, He longs for our love because His love for us is intense. You may be thinking that He doesn't know what you are really like. But He does, for God knows you intimately. We don't have to try to make Him understand. He sees deep down to the most personal thoughts and intentions of our hearts. He knows every longing we have. Hebrews 4:13 tells us that He knows every weakness, every flaw and every sin. That could be intimidating, right? But two verses later we read that he understands our weaknesses (Hebrews 4:15). GOD UNDERSTANDS!

> *As a father has compassion on his children, so the Lord has compassion on those who fear him, for he knows how we are formed, he remembers that we are dust* Psalm 103:13-14).

Isn't that great?! He does not expect a perfect performance from us. He knows we're dust. He feels with us, and His heart is pained when we go through struggles. He hurts when we hurt.

God's love includes delight and pleasure in those He loves. Think about this: By choosing to love us in an intense and personal way, God made himself vulnerable. J.I. Packer writes: "Through setting his love on men, God has voluntarily bound up his own final happiness with theirs. He will not know perfect and unmixed happiness again until He has brought every one of them to heaven."[4]

God's pleasure is linked with ours. We can bring Him joy, or we can grieve Him. Isn't it exciting to be that important to the Supreme Being of the universe?

> *The Lord your God is with you, he is mighty to save. He will take great delight in you, he will quiet you with his love, he will rejoice over you with singing* (Zephaniah 3:17)

There are so many things one could say about God's love:
    It is filled with good will and benevolent action.
    It will never fade.
    It's not something we can or have to earn.

HE IS SO PROUD OF YOU!

What I have come to understand is that not only is His creation staggering, but the reality of His love also is staggering. It recently struck me that God is proud of me!

It is difficult for us to grasp that God is proud of us. Like a father is proud of his son or daughter, so our Father God is proud of us. We might rightly respond; "What is there to be proud of? I have never done anything significant. I am not famous, I have never written a book or composed a song. I do not paint or write poetry. I do not know how to build anything with my hands, fix the car or grow a garden. All the houseplants my friends give me soon die, though not for lack of trying. What's to be proud of?"

In his book *The Ragamuffin Gospel*, Brennan Manning writes from God's perspective: "Has it crossed your mind that I am proud you accepted the gift of faith I offered you? Proud that you freely chose me, after I had chosen you, as your Friend and Lord? Proud that with all your warts and wrinkles you haven't given up? Proud that you believe in me enough to try again and again?"[5]

Wow, can you get a hold of this? He is looking at you through the eyes of a father looking at his child and saying, "I am so proud of you! You have accepted what I have offered, and you do not give up but keep trying again and again. That is so great! Do you know how it makes me feel that you want me? Do you know how much it means to me to see the hours you spend trying to learn more about me - your singing, praying, sitting quietly just to be with me? Do you know how proud it makes me feel that you *want* to be with me? All the things you could be doing and you chose freely to spend time with me. I know you have sins and struggles. I know that you are not where you feel you need to be for me to love and accept you. But I still love you and I am proud of you!"

We may not know how to handle the love and pride of a father for whom we do not have to do anything. If you were fortunate enough to grow up in a home with loving parents, then you know that from the time you were born they were proud of you. Proud of your first steps. Proud of those crayon squiggles on paper that were taped up on the walls like Rembrandt paintings. Proud of you when you came running into the room to show them your latest Play-Doh masterpiece. You knew they accepted you even when you failed again and again. You did not have to prove anything to them. You knew that there was nothing that would keep them from loving you no matter how often you ran from them and hid in your shame and embarrassment. And our Lord loves us even more than our parents.

I remember a time when one of our sons was in the midst of serious rebellion. As his parents we could not stop him from doing those things that we knew could potentially destroy him. But we could love him. During one of those moments he screamed at us in frustration, "The problem is that you love me too much! Why can't you be like my friends' parents who don't care what they do?" He was actually frustrated because no matter what he did we never stopped loving him. That love was causing him guilt and frustration, because it would have been much easier for him to rebel if we had simply rejected him. But we could not do that, and that love eventually paid off.

Your Father God is proud of you because you are His and He quite simply loves you. He understands all of your humanness. Take it into your heart and your soul: Father God is proud of you! Do not try to analyze, understand or "live up" to anything you think will make Him proud because it is not what you do but, rather, what you are. You are His. Believe it, accept it and live in the glorious freedom of it!

HIS LOVE IS AVAILABLE

God's love is available to us, but it's ours to experience only to the degree that we get involved with God. If we settle for a casual and shallow relationship, we'll block or hinder the depth to which He can go with us.

Any close relationship takes time and energy. It won't become a deep relationship if only one person is interested, while the other is indifferent or has barriers up. It won't become a deep relationship if we don't make the effort to spend time together. It takes a willingness to listen and share our hearts, and time to learn trust.

If you have dreamed of a relationship that would meet your deepest needs at every point in life, that's what God offers. Whether you are willing to take the time that is necessary is entirely up to you. But know that God is more than willing.

WE NEED TO BE AVAILABLE

Sometimes we miss the connection with God simply because it does not come in the form we think it should. I do not know the author of this poem, but it speaks volumes to the numerous ways in which God tries to communicate with us and how easily we miss hearing Him because we are expecting His answer in a specific way.

> **God Are You There?**
> The young man whispered, "God, speak to me,"
> And a meadowlark sang, but the man did not hear.
> So the young man yelled, "God, speak to me!"

And the thunder rolled across the sky, but the man did not listen.
Then he looked around and said, "God let me see you,"
And a star shone brightly, but the man did not notice.
And the man shouted, "God show me a miracle!"
And a life was born, but the man did not know.
So the man cried out in despair, "Touch me God,
And let me know you are there!"
Whereupon God reached down and touched him,
But the young man brushed the butterfly away
And walked away unknowingly. (Author unknown)

If God is seeking, drawing and persuading us to come to Him, our responsibility is to be available. To be available is to make time to be with God. No matter how badly you want to develop a relationship with someone, unless the person is available to you, it is not going to happen. Can you imagine what it would be like to try to develop an intimate relationship with someone who was never there, who was always busy? God sent His Son not only to redeem us but also to restore relationship with Him. Therefore, we have a responsibility to be in a place where God can seek, draw and persuade us; to be where we can respond.

A.W. Tozer shares that, "The important thing about a man is not where he goes when he is compelled to go, but where he goes when he is free to go where he will."[6] Just as you cannot listen to two people talking at the same time; you cannot listen to the voice of God and the voice of the world.

How often do you go to a place where you can be with God? If we are never in a place where we can respond to God, then we will not have intimacy with Him.

LIGHTEN UP - YOU'RE WAY TOO SERIOUS!

Having been around Christians most of my life I can safely say that we are a serious bunch. I believe that part of this is that we feel our value is based on what we do, not who we are. We feel that we must constantly be doing something for God in order for Him to be happy with us. Or we easily fall into the trap of taking ourselves too seriously and taking God too seriously. As if he doesn't have a sense of humor or wouldn't enjoy being around us because he just simply likes being around us. We may struggle with insecurity in our relationship with Him, knowing that we have a destiny but not knowing how to fulfill it.

As I was talking with a friend of mine, God dropped this thought into my head, "I created you to have someone to play with, someone to have fun with." That took me by surprise but as I thought about it I realized God was giving me another reason why relationship and intimacy is so important to him.

Because we often take God so seriously we forget he also laughs, has a sense of humor and thoroughly enjoys having fun. How do I know this? I mean come on, look at some of the wacky-looking creatures he created. Who can't look at a duck-billed platypus and not laugh? What about those silly looking penguins when they walk? Or, what's more ridiculous-looking than an ostrich?

MOTTO TO LIVE BY

I read this quote on a plaque I saw in a friend's office. I know it's a bit silly but it struck me as a tongue-in-cheek jab at how much time, money and energy we, especially in the United States, spend worrying about how well our bodies look.

> "Life should NOT be a journey to the grave with the intention of arriving safely in an attractive and well preserved body, but rather to skid in sideways, chocolate in one hand, latte in the other, body thoroughly used up, totally worn out, and screaming, WOO HOO, what a ride!"[7]

How about Jesus? He says that He is the exact representation of his Father. And that if you want to know what God is like, look at Him. Look how He is described in the Bible. Granted He was on a mission and it was serious. He was dealing with people that were sick, hurting and broken. But He was also human and if you dig a bit in scripture and think about His humanity it's clear that He also liked to have fun. He hung with a group of guys that were not religious prudes. Most of these men were not well-educated;

they were what we would describe as blue-collar workers. I cannot picture Him walking around looking like He was sucking on lemons.

Anyway, part of what I believe God is saying is, "You need to lighten up." We have so shrouded Him with mystery and awe that perhaps that's part of the reason He sent Jesus to show us that He does enjoy hanging with us, having fun with us and just being a friend. Abraham was called a friend of God. When I think about a friend, I think about someone I like being with. We laugh, we cry, we goof off. There are times we are serious and times we are silly. I realize that this kind of talk may upset some religious folks but we have way too much of that kind of thinking.

I completely understand that we must hold God in reverence and awe. He is worthy of our worship and trust. We must honor and respect Him. But if He is truly my friend then that relationship must have some other elements if it is going to be what I understand to be friendship.

I also thought about what it means to have fun with God, to play. Some of my most fun times are when I am out in His creation enjoying the sun, swimming, feeling the sand between my toes, the breeze gently blowing across my body as I lay in the sun listening to the sounds of the river. Also, when I pray with people and see them healed. How fun is that? God doesn't need me to do that, He can heal them without me but He lets me be a part, to participate along with Him. That's stunning!

In Genesis we read that after He finished creating this world He said, "Let us make man in our image, after our likeness." Nothing else in all of creation is quite like us. Why is that? I think in part it's because He wanted someone around who would enjoy what He had made and enjoy being with Him.

Why do we have children? Isn't it in part because we love having them around, watching them grow, doing things with them. Sure, sometimes they are a real pain but often the good things outweigh the bad and we wouldn't trade them for anything (except a little peace and quiet now and then).

The idea that the Creator of the Universe would permit us to come into His presence should fill us with a sense of gratitude, awe and reverence. This is an indication of His intensely personal love for us.

Here's something to consider; if God created you to play with, to have fun with, how would you do that? Think about what is fun or how you have fun with your friends?

As I thought about this I believe that God was reminding me to remember to lighten up a little bit and enjoy this relationship. What might He be saying to you?

THE RECOVERY OF INTIMACY

We were created for an intimate relationship with God and one another. Such a relationship indicates a life free of baggage. To be intimate means to have close association, contact or familiarity. If we were created for intimacy with God and one another, what are the identifiable signs that we are accomplishing the purpose for which we were born?

Do you remember in the earliest stages of your walk with the Lord when there was an excitement and anticipation about everything you were doing? You looked forward to going to church or being with other believers in worshipping, reading your Bible and doing things together with your believing friends. But somewhere along the way the fire died. Prayer, church attendance and witnessing are all done with little excitement, if they are done at all. You wonder what happened to the fire, anticipation and intimacy.

I was converted as a young boy of twelve and initially there was a great deal of excitement. Soon that wore off and for many years church became a place of ritual obedience. I went because I was expected to go, it was what we did. First I went to church because my parents took me then later I went because there were girls there and it was a good place to hang out with friends. At about 16 years of age I lost all interest except for the summer church camps, which were great fun. Between the ages of sixteen and twenty-five my beliefs had little effect on my lifestyle. It wasn't until I was about twenty-five that I had a spiritual encounter with God that totally affected my life and caused me to want to work on restoring that relationship with God that had become so dry and unfulfilling.

I remember coming home one weekend and sharing with a close friend that I was having difficulty even believing that God existed much less cared about us or what we were doing. My friend Bob listened patiently then wisely suggested that we pray. I was somewhat skeptical but decided why not, what could it hurt? As we bowed our heads I prayed, "God if you are real I need to know it." Suddenly I physically felt this warm wind rush from the top of my head over my body. I remember looking up at Bob and saying, "Wow, did you feel that? What was that?" He smiled and said that it was God answering my prayer. That was such a significant moment in my life that it changed forever my walk with God. I was back on a road to intimacy with God.

INTIMACY IS ROOTED IN HONESTY

Why do we try to hide from God what we are or have done? We think He will love us only if we are good, so we pretend we are something we are not. We put up a front that says to all those around us that everything is great. But on the inside we are a tangled mess of ambitions and frustrations, mingled with memories of past failures and fears of the future. We are good at being impostors.

What the Lord wants is for you to allow Him to get beneath the surface that we portray to the world to the person who lives inside your skin. It's tragic that we can profess Christ as Savior without allowing Him to be Lord of our innermost thoughts, dreams, and plans.

In I John 1:6,7 we read, *If we claim to have fellowship with him yet walk in the darkness, we lie and do not live by the truth. But if we walk in the light as he is in the light, we have fellowship with one another, and the blood of Jesus, his Son, purifies us from all sin.*

If we are "walking in the dark" we are not allowing the Lord's light of truth to reveal an area of our life and transform it from an area of stumbling and weakness into an area of power and life.

I said earlier that intimacy is rooted in honesty. Honesty with God means inviting him to take charge of all our relationships. It means recognizing our baggage and taking the steps I've laid out in previous chapters to deal with it. It means opening to Him our career, money, self-image, hopes, disappointments, dreams, and goals. If we have never been this open and honest with Him, our Christianity is a sham. That's one reason for the lack of power in many Christians today that results in dull, bland churches.

There's no lack of people who say they believe in Christ. Why then is impotence the condition of so many Christians? Has the Church made any significant impact on the direction of the United States in the last several years? If we were honest with ourselves the answer would be a resounding NO! I believe it to be in part because we have lost intimacy, lost our first love. We need His light to illuminate our memories, our hidden thoughts, and secret desires in order for there to be healing and redirection. We need His light and power in our lives to live a life that does make a difference. One man or woman can change the course of culture; can change the way an entire world communicates with each other. A modern day example would be Steve Jobs, the founder of Apple. This man has had an impact on history just as significantly as men like Thomas Edison or Henry Ford.

We ourselves are the greatest impediment to intimacy. We do the same thing with people that we have done with God. We think we will be accepted and loved only if we measure up. So we pretend we are something we are not. By doing this we not only keep out others but we deny God access to our hearts, and this impedes or stops the development of an intimate relationship with Him.

If there has been a lack of intimacy, how do we recover it? Perhaps you could start by asking yourself this: "Have I allowed God to know me absolutely and utterly? Does He know my plans, dreams and hopes for the future, or my thoughts, doubts and frustrations?" The obvious answer is of course He does because He is God! Well then, you might ask, "Why do I need to talk to Him about them?" Because when you, by a direct act of your will choose to open up and surrender these areas to God you are allowing Him to come into your life and help you fulfill those areas that are very close to your heart and are an important part of who and what you are.

There comes a time when we can't say we love God and exclude him from the real person inside. Until we allow him access to the center of our secret thoughts and feelings, there will not be intimacy. If it is unforgiveness and we admit that is what keeps us from the intimacy we were created to experience, then forgiveness is given immediately!

Can you imagine the tragedy of living your whole life under the burden of guilt, shame and anger when the experience of liberating love and forgiveness is easily obtained? It's like sitting around cursing the darkness when all you need to do is turn on a flashlight!

Perhaps you need to ask yourself, "Do I trust Him completely? Can I be totally open with Him about my feelings? Am I really sure that He will love me no matter what I say or do?"

This is why, in earlier chapters, I have urged total honesty about your inner being, whether regarding unforgiveness, low self-image, curses, soul ties - whatever the baggage.

Intimacy requires that we be vulnerable, accountable. Most of us don't like being accountable to anybody for anything. But those types of relationships are usually not very deep and don't produce growth or change. God wants an intimate relationship with you, in fact that is why He created you.

COFFEE WITH GOD

Yes, you read it right. I enjoy coffee with God and He enjoys just being with me. I know that we both look forward to this time because it gives us some time to sit together and just enjoy a good cup of java and hang out. Kind of like friends would do. Interesting thought, isn't it?

My journey with God for much of my life was centered around reading a short devotional, offering a quick prayer for my day and then some prayer for others. I was certain this kept God happy and kept me in good standing with Him. What more could He want? I was reading the Bible, tithing, attending church and praying.

We are a busy people, harried and hurried through each day. The disciplines of silence, solitude and stillness are contrary to how we live. We think that we don't have time for this or even that it is a waste of time. Francis Frangipane wrote, "He who would find God will find time."[1] Don't we always find time for the things that are important to us?

We are also an impatient people who don't like to wait. I was on a flight home from Houston with a quick stopover in Phoenix before another short hop to my home airport in Bakersfield, California. My first flight was late and I assumed since I was catching the same airline in Phoenix on to my home that they would wait a short time for me. This airline never runs on time so it was very normal to be late. I was only six minutes late arriving at my mid-stop and I bolted off the plane running to catch my next flight. As I go skidding up to the counter this sweet flight attendant says, "Sorry, we knew you were coming but we couldn't hold the plane so you will have to wait three hours for the next flight." I almost lost it.

Fortunately, instead of yelling at her, I left the counter and began walking around the terminal fuming and mumbling, "Your stupid airline is always late, you couldn't hold the plane six minutes when you knew I was coming? This is a one hour flight and now I have to wait three hours for your next flight which means I won't be home for another four hours." Finally I decided to sit down, put on my headphones and listen to some music. The song that started playing was *Bridge Over Troubled Water* by Simon and Garfunkel. "When you're weary feeling small, when tears are in your eyes I will dry them all, I'm on your side when times get rough and friends just can't be found...." As I listened to these words God said, "Michael, look at yourself, you are acting like a spoiled child. Get over it!" I started laughing at myself because I was acting as if this delay was the biggest deal in the world. Dutch Sheets says, "We don't wait well. We're into microwaving; God on the other hand is usually into marinating."[2]

Some years back I discovered that God wants to hang out with me. He wants me to relax and enjoy some free time of friendship with Him. The best way to do this for me was early in the morning. I always get up to have coffee and take a few minutes to wake up. It was quite easy to utilize this time to spend with God. I knew the importance of having a devotional time and I was occasionally good about having my quiet time with God, but I never seriously thought about just hanging out with Him. When I do this I have no agenda other than to be there with Him. For me this is the best way to hear from God.

People will often ask me, "How do you hear from God?" First of all I need to know that it is God I am hearing. This requires that I be familiar enough with His voice that I recognize His voice when He speaks. God does not speak to me in an audible voice but normally He places thoughts in my mind. Sometimes it's a word or a simple sentence. Occasionally it will be a picture. Because I have cultivated a relationship with Him, in these times of intimacy, I recognize His voice.

My wife Jane and I have been married for over forty-four years. We have a deep relationship as a result of our time together. Because of this I know her voice. When I call her on the phone I don't have to remind her that I am her husband Mike. She knows my voice. In the same way, I know God's voice because I have made a conscious effort to spend time with Him doing nothing but just being with Him. Jane and I can be in the same room and we don't have to talk, we just enjoy being with one another. That's the type of relationship God wants with us.

Do you have a friend that you enjoy being with? Why not have that same relationship with God? He wants to have that deep friendship with you. If I want to become someone's friend I must spend time with them. Some of the time we do an activity but much of the time we just enjoy being with each other.

When we have our devotional time or our special quiet time with God usually we have an agenda. We want to hear from Him or we want an answer, some direction or affirmation. What if you had a friend and you knew that every time he came to spend time with you, he wanted something from you. No matter what reason he gave for being there, you knew there was always some other purpose. How would that make you feel? Isn't that what we often do to God? Did you ever think that occasionally He would like to be with us when we don't want something from Him? Think about this, wouldn't it be nice if you could just hang out with your friend knowing that there was no agenda other than that they just liked being with you?

I believe it's difficult for us to do this because many of us have been conditioned by our culture to stay busy. If we aren't doing something we are wasting time. Wasting time is not looked upon favorably. Even when we are with people we love we are busy doing or thinking about something else. Consider this; how would you feel as a parent if during a typical seven-day week your grown child came to your house to spend an hour with you? This was your special time together. What if during that hour they talked with you while reading the newspaper, watching television or texting their friends? At the end of the hour they jumped up, gave you a hug, said, "See you next week," and headed out the door.

If that's the only time you get with them the entire week would you be immensely pleased and thankful that they had spent time with you? Would you consider that quality time? I suspect that while you would be happy to see them and grateful for what little time they did give you, wouldn't you also be a little saddened? There was so much you wanted to share with them but there just wasn't enough time. Isn't that typical of how many of us spend our time with God?

How do you see God? Often, we unwittingly project onto God our own attitudes and feelings toward ourselves. As Brennan Manning says, "God made man in his own image and man returned the compliment."[3] Thus if we feel hateful toward ourselves, we assume that God feels hateful toward us. But we cannot assume that He feels about us the way we feel about ourselves unless we love ourselves compassionately, intensely, freely.

Perhaps we believe we are of little worth to God, we are too bad to be forgiven or we must work to earn his love. It's nonsense to believe this because we limit what God can do with us. To quote Manning again, "We deem ourselves too inconsiderable to be used even by a God capable of miracles with no more than mud and spit."[4]

If you have lost that sense of intimate connection with God or perhaps have never had it, you can choose now to change all that. But first you must come to accept that merely being with God has immense value. Theologian Edward Schillebeeckx wrote, "In a revealed religion, silence with God has value in itself and for its own sake, just because God is God. Failure to recognize the value of mere being with God, as the beloved, without doing anything is to gouge the heart out of Christianity."[5] To gouge the heart out… That's stunning!

Part of moving to this place with God is to love ourselves. If we fear God, we cannot accept love from God. If we cannot accept love from God, we cannot love ourselves or others. If we cannot accept ourselves in both our strengths and weaknesses, we cannot accept that we are of value to God. To grasp the reality of being God's Beloved is totally beyond our reach. Someone once said, "The sorrow of God lies in our fear of Him, our fear of life, and our fear of ourselves."

What are the benefits of intimacy with God? A peace begins to settle over your whole being. You start to grasp how special you are to Him. The haste and driven pace at which most of us live begins to lessen. Your dependence for approval from man becomes less and less of an issue. The desire for the spotlight fades. You want to be alone because you start to hunger for and enjoy the solitude and silence. You start to see, smell and hear the world around you in a new way. You begin to see others with new eyes. Furthermore, there is an appreciation for every moment of every day. The fears associated with the future become smaller. There is a fresh passion for God and the things of God. There's a new level of peace in your spirit. You become more at peace with yourself. You begin to realize that God's approval does not depend on what you do or don't do.

I discovered that the benefits of hanging out with God far outweigh what I thought was consuming so much of my valuable time. That thinking, in and of itself is absurd. We are after all, with the God of the universe!

He wants to be a friend. While I hunger to have an intimate relationship with God as my Abba, ("Daddy "in Aramaic), I also need to see Him as friend, one with whom I can be myself and know that He understands and accepts me in my humanness. When I understand that He accepts me, then I can begin to grasp my uniqueness and destiny as a child of eternity.

WHAT IS A FRIEND?

One of the most beautiful definitions of a friend was a piece I read many years ago by C. Raymond Beran. "It is a person with whom you dare to be yourself. Your soul can be naked with him. He seems to ask of you to put on nothing, only to be what you are. He does not want you to be better or worse. When you are with him, you feel as a prisoner feels who has been declared innocent. You do not have to be on your guard. You can say what you think, so long as it is genuinely you. He understands those contradictions in your nature that lead others to misjudge you. With him you breathe freely. You can avow your little vanities and envies and hates and vicious sparks your meannesses and absurdities and, in opening them up to him, they are lost, dissolved on the white ocean of his loyalty. He understands, you do not have to be careful. You can abuse him, neglect him, tolerate him. Best of all, you can keep still with him. It makes no matter. He likes you. He is like fire that purges to the bone. He understands. You can weep with him, laugh with him, pray with him. He sees, knows and loves you. "A friend? What is a friend? Just one, I repeat, with whom you dare to be yourself."[6]

As you embark on this journey find ways to have some time for coffee with God. It's not a difficult thing to do. You will discover that He is proud of you, wants to be your friend and you will experience what it means to be His beloved.

Consider this: The God who created the universe, who heals the sick, who knows you need food and shelter to survive, against whom all military might and power is but a puff of dust, beside whose power a swirling, raging river is but a trickle in the sand, is the God who wants to spend time **with you.**

GOD'S HIGHEST PURPOSE

In the book of Luke is a passage that for me describes what I believe to be our mandate as believers. It reads, *The Spirit of the Lord is on me, because he has anointed me to preach good news to the poor. He has sent me to proclaim freedom for the prisoners and recovery of sight for the blind, to release the oppressed, to proclaim the year of the Lord's favor* (Luke 4:18-19). If you recall, this is the passage from the Old Testament that Jesus read publicly in a synagogue and claimed as the mandate the Father had sent Him to accomplish. If we are to do what Jesus did, then this is also our mandate or as I like to call it, our Job Description.

The Gospel at its simplest is doing what Jesus did. While I strongly believe that God created us for relationship with Him and that part of His purpose is for us to spread the Good News, I would submit that God's Highest Purpose for us is Christ-likeness.

Obviously there will be opposition from our enemy. We know that Satan will engage us in spiritual warfare. Most of us are familiar with physical healing, repentance, inner healing, deliverance, and spiritual warfare. Any one of these can become our primary focus. But, if indeed God's highest purpose is to bring us into the image of Jesus Christ, then He must be our focus at all times. Did God deliver us out of sin to go along on our merry way and live for ourselves? NO! He delivered us out of sin that we might become like Christ.

In Romans we read, *And we know that in all things God works for the good of those who love him, who have been called according to His purpose. For those God foreknew He also predestined to be conformed to the likeness of His Son, that He might be the firstborn among many brothers (Romans 8:28, 29).*

The specific purpose, toward which God steers the working of all things in our lives, is our conformity to His Son Jesus. The Father's purpose in our salvation was that Jesus would become "the first-born- among many brethren." In other words, the way to realize God's ultimate victory is to reach toward His ultimate goal, which is complete transformation into the likeness of Christ.

There is a book by Francis Frangipane titled *The Three Battlegrounds*. I want to quote some from that book because he simply says it much better than I could.

"There is a penetration of spirit between God and ourselves, where our spirits are fully saturated with the Living Presence of the Lord Jesus, where His glory so floods our lives that there is ...NO DARK PART...left within us (Luke 11:36). This immediacy of the Lord's presence produces an indestructible defense, a fortress within which we are hidden from evil. Through Him, we enter the excellence of His ways in our relationships, both with the Father and one another; thereby walking in immunity from countless satanic attacks. Indeed, as His fullness within us increases, then that which is written is fulfilled: *"He who is born of God keeps us safe and the evil one does not touch us"*(I John 5:18). [1]

To perfectly subdue the devil we must walk in the "shelter of the Most High." *He who dwells in the shelter of the Most High will rest in the shadow of the Almighty* (Psalm 91:1). Satan is tolerated for one purpose: the warfare between the devil and God's saints thrusts us into Christ-likeness, where the nature of Christ becomes our only place of rest and security. God allows warfare to facilitate His eternal plan, which is to make people in the image of His Son.

SIN - THAT'S THE ONLY THING I KNOW HOW TO DO!

You may respond that you understand God's desire is for you to become Christ-like, but Christ did not sin. But I, on the other hand, would respond, "Sin? That's the only thing we know how to do!" That is so much a part of our nature that we don't have to be taught how to do it. It comes quite naturally and easily for me and for you. What we must realize is that it is not Satan who defeats us; it is our openness to him. I was reading Brother Lawrence one day and came across a statement he made regarding sin. When asked about sin he said,

"That's the only thing I know how to do!"[2] As I read on, it became clear that he was recognizing and accepting that sin was in his basic nature.

We don't have to be taught how to sin. From birth we are being taught something. We are shown how to walk, read, hold our spoon, or drink from a cup, basic skills we need to get along in this world. But nobody has to teach us how to sin. We know that from birth. We get angry, rebellious and envious or display any number of behaviors accepting that we are by nature sinful creatures. We deny, hide, run from or make excuses for our sinful behavior. Finding it difficult to accept our humanness we put on masks that we wear before people and before God because we think that if they really knew us they would reject us. This inability to accept our basic nature keeps us from God. That is the tragedy.

Andrew Murray in his book *Absolute Surrender* wrote, "Why is a lamb so gentle?" Because that is its nature. Does it cost the lamb any trouble to be gentle? No. Why not? Does a lamb study to be gentle? No. Why does that come so easy? That is its nature. And a wolf-why does it cost a wolf no trouble to be cruel? Because that is its nature. It doesn't have to summon up its courage; the cruel nature is there. You can be cruel to a lamb and it will remain gentle. Or, you can be gentle to a wolf and it will still be cruel."[3]

If God's second greatest commandment is, "Love your neighbor as you love yourself," don't you think He understood we were sinful creatures and that we would always be sinful creatures? Do you think that knowledge keeps Him from loving us? Often, we cannot accept our own sinful nature and thus we find it difficult to love ourselves. If we cannot accept ourselves, we cannot accept others. Even more tragic is that we cannot accept love from God. If I can understand and accept that it is in my nature to sin, then I can begin to do those things that help deal with the sin. Instead of the sin keeping me from God, it drives me *to* God.

I have discovered that accepting my humanity and knowing that I am going to sin, make mistakes and fail, helps me to quickly deal with my sin and humbly go before my Father where I know there is acceptance and forgiveness. We did not need anyone to teach us how to sin, but we do need God to teach us how to love and accept ourselves. Let's determine to not let our basic nature keep us from God but to drive us to God.

Once we realize that the Father's goal is to transform our lives with Christ's life, we will continually find that God has one answer to spiritual warfare and that is to appropriate - that is, take to ourselves as our possession - the nature of His Son! Are you troubled by demons of fear or doubt? Submit those areas to God, repenting of your unbelief and then yielding yourself to Christ's faith within you. Are you troubled with spirits of lust and shame? Present those very areas of sin to God, repenting of your old nature, drawing upon the forgiveness of Christ and His purity of heart.

The Father is more concerned with the coming forth of His Son in our lives than He is in defeating Satan. Who is the devil, that he can defy the Living God? Indeed, it is of the greatest truth that, once the devil recognizes his assault against your life has not pulled you from God, but toward Him, once he perceives that his temptations are actually forcing you to appropriate the virtue of Christ, the enemy will withdraw!

In his book, *Wild At Heart*, John Eldridge wrote, "God created you to be his intimate ally, to join Him in the Great Battle. You have a specific place in the line, a mission God made you for. There is no other man who can replace you in your life. If you leave your place in the line, it will remain empty. No one else can be who you are meant to be. You are the hero in your story."[4]

BEHOLD AND BEWARE! HERE WALKS A CHILD OF GOD!

Can you imagine what your life would be like if you began to fully grasp that the Spirit of God, the Creator of the Universe, lives in you? Scripture says, *Don't you realize that all of you together are the temple of God and that the Spirit of God lives I you?* (1 Corinthians 3:16, NLT). If the Spirit of God dwells in us, then what difference should it make in our lives? Let me suggest some things you might want to consider.

First, if He is dwelling within doesn't it make sense that He wants relationship with us? Though we may be comfortable with religion, rituals and rules, relationships often make us nervous. Relationships require work. Deep, long lasting relationships require honesty, transparency and intimacy. It's the Spirit of God touching and dwelling with our human spirit. It's a bit staggering to think that God has called us to Himself and wants to reveal Himself to us and then through us to others. That He wants to have the same level of intimacy with us that He had with His Son Jesus.

Second, one thing that made Jesus unique was his quality of life. If we began to live the quality of life Jesus had we would likely begin to believe like Jesus. He knew that sickness was not from God and that when He prayed for people they would be healed! His faith was such that nothing was impossible for Him. When food was needed, food was provided. When demons needed to be cast out or dead sons and daughters brought back to life it was simply done. Not a big deal to Jesus! Why? Because of his faith. He knew He was loved, He knew His identity, He knew His destiny. In Scripture it says we are destined to become like Christ. I believe this promise is not just for the hereafter but for now as well. If we lived this quality of life our lives would dramatically change.

Third, if God's Spirit is truly within us and in complete control of our lives, demons would tremble at our arrival. How do you appear to angels or demons? Some years ago I was on a ministry trip to Banff, Canada. At that time I was naïve in regards to witchcraft, demons and their various activities. I was not aware of it at the time but one of the people at the camp brought along a young girl who was a practicing witch. She brought her hoping that she would be converted and leave the practice of witchcraft behind.

What puzzled me about this girl was that she always avoided me. When I would be walking across the camp she would see me and go out of her way to avoid me. I found that behavior a bit odd and asked her friend why she was acting so strange. Her reply was, "She knows that the power within you is stronger than the power that is within her!" With her spiritual perception she recognized within me God's presence. While I understood this intellectually I did not grasp spiritually the significance of being a child of God. That was an eye opener for me. I understand much better now that wherever I go, the Spirit of God goes. Therefore, if the spirit of God goes with me, then wherever I go I can walk in the confidence of a Son or Daughter of the King, assured that he is indeed with me. How do you appear to the spirit-world? I want them to see me and exclaim, "Behold and beware! Here walks a Child of God!"

THANK YOU FOR REMINDING ME

I remember at some point in my journey I was trying to white knuckle my way through a specific temptation that had plagued me for years. I sensed the Lord saying to me, "Michael, whenever Satan brings that temptation to you let it remind you that you need to immediately bring it to me. Say to Satan, 'Thank you for reminding me how weak I am and that I need to pray for God's strength right now!'" When I started doing this I found that it not only irritated Satan, but he quit tempting me in that area because every time he tempted me it reminded me to pray, which made me stronger in resisting that temptation.

We are not called to focus on the battle or the devil, except where that battle hinders our immediate transformation into Christ's likeness. Our calling is to focus on Jesus. The work of the devil, however, is to draw our eyes from Jesus. Satan's first weapon always involves luring our eyes from Christ. Remember that temptation is one of his most potent weapons. Turn to Jesus and almost immediately the battle vanishes.

There is a time when the Lord will call us to pull down strongholds, to confront evil and rebuke it in the name of Jesus. There is a time when we will enter into intense spiritual warfare. But it must never become our focus. If God's purpose is to bring us into the image of Christ, nothing, not worship nor warfare, neither love nor deliverance, is truly attainable if we miss the singular objective of our faith: Christ- likeness.

We must learn that, on a personal level, it is better to develop godly virtues than to spend our day praying against the devil. Indeed, it is the joy of the Lord that casts out spirits of depression. It is our living faith that destroys spirits of unbelief. It is aggressive love that casts out fear.

ON EARTH AS IT IS IN HEAVEN!

I was listening to an acquaintance of mine teach on healing. When I first heard him say, "We don't have to tolerate this," it rocked me back a bit as I began to catch the implications of what he was talking about. His topic was praying for healing with authority and a Kingdom of God mentality. His thesis being that we are a people of God's Kingdom, put on earth as Ambassadors of that Kingdom, with a specific responsibility to bring in the Kingdom of God, "On earth as it is in heaven." He pointed out that the Kingdom of God has everything in it that everybody wants and needs. In this Kingdom in order to live you die. In order to gain you lose. In order to receive you give, in order to be lifted up you lie low. It's the nature of this Kingdom. Jesus knew that this Kingdom that He came to bring brought deliverance and healing. There is a reality that is far superior to what we can see, taste and touch. It is a reality that is invisible to our natural eyes. And we are called to bring in this Kingdom reality.

In Matthew Jesus says, *But seek first His Kingdom and His righteousness and all these things will be given to you as well* (Matthew 6:33). If we seek His Kingdom, we'll find that it comes with everything we need. It brings with it His answer to our material and relational needs and our fight against evil. In the Kingdom of God there is no sickness, there is no bitterness, hopelessness, lack or any of a number of things we experience here on earth.

If we are Ambassadors of another Kingdom, and if that Kingdom has everything we need, and if we are to reach out and bring in that Kingdom, and represent that Kingdom wherever we go, why is there rampant poverty? Why are drugs, sex and rebellion running uncontrolled among our children? Why is there such sickness and disease all around us?

I believe there are several reasons. Though I am not able to deal with all of them here there are some that I can address. In part we are overwhelmed. Many of us have been faithful to pray for people for years without seeing any change and we've become discouraged. Some of us have felt inadequate, inexperienced or ill equipped. Or, we are quite simply overwhelmed with trying to deal with the frantic pace of our daily lives.

But I also believe it's because we don't truly understand who we are, what we've been called to do and what we have available to do it with. The Word of God says we are His beloved, that we are to seek first His Kingdom and that all authority in heaven and on earth has been given to us. It tells us that we are of immense value, that in the Kingdom of God is all that we will ever need, and that we have the authority to see that Kingdom established here on earth. Our responsibility is to believe this and be available to do it.

Are people hungry for this Kingdom? I think the answer to that question is obvious. During the last thirty plus years of my life, I watched as people flocked to wherever God was moving. In the early 1980's it was to Anaheim and the Vineyard, in the 90's it was to Toronto and Brownsville. Now we are seeing fires of revival and renewal starting in numerous places around the world.

During the time of Jesus, wherever He was, people left their jobs, their homes and walked great distances to find this man that was doing things beyond their wildest imagination. They were so desperate that they left everything that they had going on in their life. They abandoned all of it, grabbed every sick person they could and took them to Jesus. We get happy and excited when we see one person healed. Multiply that hundreds of times in seeing families restored and people healed of all kinds of sickness and disease. They didn't have to be told to get happy, they were happy. They were experiencing the joy of the Lord. It wasn't something they sang about, it was something they saw and felt. Why? Because Jesus didn't tolerate sickness and disease and neither should we.

So, let's make it our purpose with the remaining days or years God gives us to not allow the world to beat us down. Let's rise above the weariness, compromise, discouragement, busyness or fear and purpose not to tolerate those things in our lives that we know are not a part of the Kingdom of God. Let's allow God to renew our minds and restore our spirits so that we have a Kingdom mentality that says; "I am God's beloved, I want to see His Kingdom come on earth, and I can be a part of bringing that Kingdom in." Let's purpose to move to that place of being conformed into the image of Jesus Christ. If God's highest purpose is Christ-likeness, then our hearts and minds will be set on bringing into our lives His Kingdom now!

"VICTORY BEGINS WITH THE NAME OF JESUS ON OUR LIPS. IT IS CONSUMMATED BY THE NATURE OF JESUS IN OUR HEART."[5]

WHAT GOD WILL NOT ACCEPT!

Did you ever wonder how Jesus accepted the weaknesses of His disciples who were His closest friends? For example there was the blustering, impetuous Peter, the doubting of Thomas and the deception of Judas.

How do we with our finite minds comprehend God's total, unqualified acceptance and forgiveness? Scripture seems to indicate that no matter how bad we are God will forgive and accept us.

While that may be true, there are serious consequences to sin and those consequences affect us as we live in the Kingdom now as well as for all eternity.

If we are going to live as kingdom people we must understand what God will not accept. In Mark we read, *Isaiah was right when he prophesied about you hypocrites; as it is written: "These people honor me with their lips, but their hearts are far from me. They worship me in vain; their teachings are but rules taught by men." You have let go of the commands of God and are holding on to the traditions of men* (Mark 7:6,8).

What Jesus is speaking about here is hypocrisy. At first glance you may be thinking that it is directed toward those religious leaders of His day and all their outward display of religion. You may be saying to yourself, "I'm not a hypocrite. But even if I were in some small way, it would be such a small thing as to be of no consequence." A further examination of this verse reveals that hypocrisy to God in any form is not a small thing.

Hypocrisy by definition is: the acting of a false part, pretending, a deception as to real character and feeling, especially in regard to morals and religion. A hypocrite is one who pretends to be pious and virtuous without really being so, one who pretends to be what he is not.

Before You Get Here

In Matthew we read, *How terrible it will be for you teachers of religious law and you Pharisees. Hypocrites! For you are careful to tithe even the tiniest part of your income, but you ignore the important things of the law-justice, mercy, and faith* (Matthew 23:23 NLT).

Then he moves on to how they outwardly appear righteous but inside are full of uncleanness, lawlessness and self-indulgence. Basically, He is saying, "You are concerned about fulfilling your own desires and needs, but I know you are not what you appear to be. That's hypocritical and I will not accept it!" You cannot be a part of the body of Christ as merely a spectator. If you view membership in the body of Christ as a spectator sport then you *are* involved in hypocrisy. You are pretending to be what you are not - a Christian - and God will not accept that!

In Luke 13 we read the story about Jesus in the synagogue. He had just healed a woman who had been sick for eighteen years. The religious leaders were indignant because He had violated one of their religious laws by healing her on the Sabbath. Jesus response to them was anger. He was angry because they were more concerned about their traditions than this woman, who was a child of God who had been suffering (Luke 13:10-17).

Hypocrisy shows itself in many ways. Sometimes we are dishonest with those around us when we need to be open and transparent about what is really going on with us. Some time back I knew of a brother who was going through some intense emotional and physical pain. I wanted to reach out and help him but every time we talked and I would ask him how things were his reply was, "Fine, I'm doing real well." But I knew what was going on with him inside and yet he would stand and give glowing testimonies, offer up pious prayers, and willingly volunteer his time. If you read the definition of hypocrisy he was being hypocritical by his very actions. How serious is this? The result of that behavior has been that eventually he turned his back on God, the church, and his friends and headed down a path that will eventually destroy him!

Do you remember when Jesus took his three closest friends into the garden to pray? They saw Him pleading with his Father, they saw Him in intense agony, in what could be perceived as a position of weakness. Why do you suppose He allowed them to observe Him in that way? I believe so that they could see Him as He was, totally subject to the Father's will and yet with all the weaknesses and frailties of human flesh. For Jesus to have left them outside the garden, gone in to pray, and come back out pretending everything was just fine would be hypocritical.

There's another way we get caught up in hypocrisy and it often manifests itself as religious pride. This religious pride keeps us from being real. A friend was sharing the other evening that when he was going through a particularly difficult time in his life financially that his pride kept him from reaching out for help. He couldn't even ask for prayer, for that would be to admit that he needed help. It was as if his reputation and spiritual maturity were at stake. To him to admit a need was indicative of not trusting God.

ARE YOU THE REAL THING?

There was a slogan some years back that Coca Cola used in its marketing campaign. It was, "Coke, It's The Real Thing." Whatever that means in regards to cola, we bought it and drank it knowing that it was the real thing. If you like Coke then you know when someone tries to slip in a Pepsi or other cola that it is not the real thing. In regards to your faith and walk with God are you the real thing? If you are the genuine article then those around you will notice that you are different in many ways. Perhaps they notice that there is something about you that is different but they are not sure what it is or how to explain it.

Francis Frangipane wrote, "Our experience of Christianity must go beyond just being another interpretation of the Bible; it must expand until our faith in Jesus and our love for Him becomes a lightning rod for His presence."[1]

A lightning rod attracts. It says throughout the Word that we will do the works that Jesus did. When we examine what Jesus did we see clearly that He walked in holiness and power. He spoke and people were transformed from death into life. He prayed and people were healed. People were attracted to Him. They saw what He did, and they listened to what He said. The Truth that He spoke changed those who heard it. He did not slip into the impostor role to fit in.

He was what He spoke and lived. His faith was extraordinary, His life anything but normal. He did not fake anything. People were attracted to Him because of what He said and what He did. He was the "real thing". We however, can easily fake Christianity.

We can easily pretend to be the real thing. Frangipane wrote, "If we have been indoctrinated to believe that the Kingdom of God, and Christianity itself, does not really have to work, or if the absence of holiness and power fails to trouble us, something is seriously wrong with our concept of truth."[2]

If you are not drawn to holiness, if you do not see power manifested, if your prayers are not answered, then it would seem logical to ask why. Do you expect holiness to be a part of your life as you go about your day? Do you expect your prayers to be answered? Do you expect your Christian beliefs to work? Do those around you expect these things? Does your church or small group expect these things?

We like familiarity, we like routine and we don't like to step out into unfamiliar territory and walk on the water because it's scary. It threatens our familiar and comfortable place. Peter didn't hesitate to step out of the boat, but once he realized where he was, he became afraid and wanted to get back into the boat because it was familiar and safe. There is nothing wrong with the familiar, but the familiar is often too comfortable, and by nature we like comfortable. Staying comfortable with those things that are normal and ordinary often keep us from experiencing that which is extraordinary.

So, rather than move into a place of faith, expectancy and obedience, a place where we are drawn closer to knowing and loving Jesus, we compromise and slip into being impostors. Before we realize it we are not the "real thing."

Stop for a moment and consider this: If Christ is within us, we should be moving towards living holy, powerful lives; lives that attract others. No excuses! Christianity is not just accepting some doctrine, going to church regularly, being a part of a small group and faithfully paying our tithe. It is living daily in the reality of Christ's presence where we live and work.

In Philippians Paul writes, *I want to know Christ and the power of his resurrection, and the fellowship of sharing in his sufferings, becoming like him in his death, and so, somehow, to attain to the resurrection from the dead. Not that I have already obtained all this or have already been made perfect, but I press on to take hold of that for which Christ Jesus took hold of me* (Philippians 3:10). When we settle for anything less than the fullness of Christ in any part of our life we settle for less than being the real thing in all of our life.

YOU DON'T LOOK LIKE YOU'RE REDEEMED

Oral tradition from the nineteenth century tells the story of the atheist philosopher Friedrich Nietzsche who was said to have reproached a group of Christians with the words, "You make me sick!" When their spokesman asked why, Nietzsche replied, "Because you redeemed don't look like you're redeemed!"

That's a curious response isn't it? And yet, must we not stop and examine how the unbelieving view us as we live out our life of faith? Countless times I have been around believers whose countenance is such that though they may be happy and joyful inside, they haven't notified their faces because they look as if they have been sucking on lemons. I have heard people say, "If that's what being a Christian is like, I don't want to be one!"

Perhaps part of the problem lies in our understanding of who we are and what we possess. Consider this, "Are you spiritually rich or spiritually poor?" Brennan Manning makes the statement that if we consider ourselves spiritually rich we begin to make demands on God for things that we think we deserve, often leading to anger and frustration. If we presume that life owes us the best and nothing but the best, then reality rarely lives up to our expectations. What logically follows is that we take for granted everything that comes our way and bear ourselves with the swagger of the executive who knows what is up and has all under control.

To be spiritually poor is to realize that everything is a gift. Salvation, mercy, grace, provision, protection, all that comes from the hand of God is a gift. That He would love us is, in itself, irrational and unreasonable. The spiritually poor experience genuine gratitude and appreciate the slightest gift. The rich in spirit devote considerable time to thinking about what they don't have; the poor get right down to enjoying and celebrating what they *do* have.

As we stand before God with open hands, not clinging to anything, our life becomes a life of humble, joyful thanksgiving. When we begin to let go of our self-sufficiency and realize what it means to be the Beloved and that He is more than sufficient, we disappear into what Thomas Merton calls, "The immense poverty that is the adoration of God."[3] I suspect that then the redeemed will look like they're redeemed.

WE MUST DIE TO OUR IDOLS

Anything that stands between us and a deep, intimate walk with God cannot be politely tolerated. We have a jealous God. *Do not worship any other God, for the Lord, whose name is Jealous, is a jealous God* (Exodus. 34:14). This is not petty, possessive and insecure human jealousy. God's jealousy is based on His pure love for us, His desire to bless us and for us to fulfill our lives in Him. Rather than being simply a philosophical principal of "higher cosmic consciousness," He is a living, loving God who wants to be with us. Richard Foster wrote, "Today the heart of God is an open wound of love. He aches over our distance and preoccupation. He mourns that we do not draw near to Him. He grieves that we have forgotten Him. He weeps over our obsession with muchness and manyness. He longs for our presence."[4]

We must be willing to die to those values that wrongly have first place in our hearts. Modern idols keep us from spending time with God and tempt us to perversion, compromise and doubt in God's ability to protect and provide. Though we may not always understand Him or know the outcome of what He does, we must come to the point where we know that "He is able." If we are not there in our walk with Him, then we likely have some "idols" that have replaced Him in our lives.

In his book *Abba's Child*, Brennan Manning makes the case that we are all "impostors." "Fearing that people will discover who we really are and will not like us, we hide our real selves. Pride drives us to pretend we are smart when we are around the well educated. Around the wealthy, we pretend we are rich. With 'the religious folks,' we pretend to be religious. We put on a happy face, pretending we are all together and life is wonderful, when inside we are emotionally imploding. We carry this 'impostor' mentality a step further and even let it invade our relationship with God. The pursuit of money, power, glamour, sexual prowess, recognition and status enhances one's self-importance and creates the illusion of success."[5]

This facade can keep us from honesty and transparency, and we may end up merely jumping through religious hoops. All of these imposter motives are actually idols that separate us from knowing God.

And we do not want to just know God intellectually. We must allow Him to move from our heads to our hearts. As A.W. Tozer puts it, "To seek our divinity merely in books and writings is to seek the living among the dead; we do but in vain many times seek God in these, where His truth too often is not so much enshrined as entombed. Our theology of God has replaced an encounter with God, and in our hearts there is no one there."[6] To allow anything - especially any idols - to keep us from time with God is to miss the very reason God created us.

The type of transparency that will keep us from this hypocrisy is risky and requires that you be honest with yourself, others and God. How can I laugh with you when I don't know you are joyful? How can I cry with you when I don't know you are hurting or pray for you when you tell me everything is great and just getting better!?

I am not so naïve as to ask that those who read this suddenly open up and become vulnerable to each other but I would ask that you begin to examine your walk with Jesus and your desire to be real. If you never allow yourself to become vulnerable and real to either God or anyone else, you will be unable to give or receive love, acceptance and forgiveness.

I AM TOTALLY USELESS!

This sounds a bit strange doesn't it? I read this in a fascinating article titled, "Hearing God's Voice and Obeying His Word" in *Leadership* magazine. It is an interview with Richard Foster and Henry Nouwen and was written for ministers. I think it is easily applicable to all of us. The basic article is about our devotional life: spending time with God, getting to know God, listening to God and being available for God. We want to spend time with God and be used by Him, but we have so many interruptions, obligations and responsibilities that we may feel it is impossible. How do we cope with the interruptions? Here's how Nouwen answers that. "What I'm talking about is having a spiritual attitude that wants to be surprised by God. We crowd our thoughts with so many agenda items that we don't take time to listen to God. The minister in one sense is a useless person; useless in that he or she can be used at any time by any one for any thing."[7]

Let me take this from the realm of the professional minister and apply it to all of us. As believers we want to be available for God to be used by God at any time and place of His choosing. At least that's what we profess. The question is; "How do we do this?" In the same article quoted above, Henry Nouwen says; "Act totally useless, hang around people, tell them you don't want anything you just want to be with them and love them."

What he's really talking about is a spiritual attitude. Often when we are doing something for God, we see it as a task. Whether we are leading a small group, witnessing to someone in the marketplace or helping build a church in Mexico, we have a task to do and an underlying agenda. However, if we develop a spiritual attitude of anticipation, then if God wants to surprise us with something, we are available no matter what we are doing. He wants us - unequivocally, unreservedly and without pretense. That is when we become totally useless and therefore totally dependent upon Him.

We don't have to sit around waiting for God to speak to us in a burning bush. That may happen, but He also speaks to us at times when we are in the middle of doing something else. Because we have the attitude of being available to God to bless others at any time, anywhere, people begin to sense that you want to be with them, to be available to them, to love them, and then they will respond to you. It doesn't matter if they are believers or not. They will see that there is something about you that is different and they will like it. If you have times set aside to be totally useless, I believe God will surprise you. Imagine the surprise on people's faces when they ask you what you are doing and you reply, "Nothing, I am totally useless!"

UNLESS YOU CHANGE AND BECOME AS LITTLE CHILDREN...

At that time the disciples came to Jesus and asked, "Who is the greatest in the kingdom of heaven?" He called a little child and had him stand among them. And he said: "I tell you the truth, unless you change and become like little children, you will never enter the kingdom of heaven. Therefore, whoever humbles himself like this child is the greatest in the kingdom of heaven" (Matthew 18:1-4).

When we think of little children we often picture noise, movement, fussing, loud screaming, fighting, sibling rivalry, self-centeredness, selfishness, etc. Yet throughout scripture believers are referred to as children. In one of the most familiar passages in the Bible, the Beatitudes we read, *God blesses those who work for peace for they will be called the children of God* (Matthew.5:9, NLT). Further, *John writes, And now dear children, continue in him so that when he appears we may be confident and unashamed before him at his coming* (I John 2: 28).

God is not referring to children as we often refer to children nor does He desire us to become childish. I believe He was saying that one who is exhibiting trust, openness, and eagerness is childlike. And that is what He is looking for from us, childlike faith and openness.

Also, he is not saying that children are outstanding examples of humility, or any other virtue. He is pointing out that we can only possess the humility necessary for entrance into the kingdom of heaven if we are prepared to be insignificant, as little children were in the ancient world. A little child has no idea that he is great, and so in the kingdom of heaven the greatest is he who is least conscious of being great. Jesus points out that if you are prepared to be as insignificant as little children, then you can enter the kingdom of heaven.

Look with me at another example of Jesus dealing with children. *Then little children were brought to Jesus for him to place his hands on them and pray for them. But the disciples rebuked those who brought them. Jesus said, "Let the little children come to me and do not hinder them, for the kingdom of heaven belongs to such as these."* (Matthew 19:13-15) He uses this as another opportunity to teach a vital truth about the character of the members of the kingdom of God. Jesus was fully aware of the children's frailties. Nevertheless, He undoubtedly believed that though far from innocent they were more sensitive to the supernatural world than adults tend to be. It is easier for them to see God's hand directly at work in his creation, doing what adults often tend to regard as ordinary things, but which to children are matters of great significance.

Jesus is not encouraging His disciples to be childish. Jesus would rather have His disciples regain and retain those childlike qualities that are not incompatible with maturity. The kingdom of God, He implies, belongs to those who are trustful, receptive and friendly, and who remain unspoiled by the difficulties and disillusionments, the cynicism and the pessimism, the compromises and the deceptions that so often depress and disfigure adult life. He wants us to retain those childlike qualities that make us receptive to what the Father is saying and doing. Think about the wonder, receptiveness and unsophistication of children.

What Jesus meant is clear. A child is dependent and trusting - at least until adult unworthiness breaks the trust. A child is friendly and unconscious of status or race, until adult prejudice spoils that relationship. A child is candid, as witness the Hans Christian Andersen story of the emperor's new clothes: The adults pretended to admire the clothes, not daring to say anything different, until a little child said, "But he has nothing on!" A child lives in constant wonder, makes toys out the boxes they came in and finds life a high romance. A child expects great things of life and finds them. The faith that Jesus prized is instinct in a child.

But Jesus may also have had in mind a child's innocence. "Unless you change (turn)...." You see, the pardon of God can do what we cannot do ourselves. We can once more become childlike. Then we are trusting. Then we are candid and sincere. Then we are expectant.

MOVING BEYOND FAILURE

I know you may be familiar with this story from Matthew 26 regarding Peter's denial of knowing Jesus and his attendant failure. I want to look at this again from the perspective of the healing that Jesus walked Peter into after the failure. We don't often have a problem with God doing big things like healing the sick and raising the dead. But we do have problems when we feel we have failed miserably or we have not been faithful or bold or any number of things we do to ourselves. I want to look at the dynamics of what is happening here as Jesus takes Peter beyond the failure and back into restoration.

First let's go back to when all this started. They are all sitting around the table eating, probably really enjoying each other's company when the conversation turns serious. First of all Jesus says "one of you will betray me", then He begins talking about the bread and the wine and how they represent His body and blood. Shortly after this they go out to the Mount of Olives where this following conversation takes place.

> *Then Jesus told them, "This very night you will all fall away on account of me, for it is written: 'I will strike the shepherd, and the sheep of the flock will be scattered.' But after I have risen, I will go ahead of you into Galilee." Peter replied, "Even if all fall away on account of you, I never will." "I tell you the truth," Jesus answered, "this very night, before the rooster crows, you will disown me three times." But Peter declared, "Even if I have to die with you, I will never disown you." And all the other disciples said the same (Matthew 26-31-35).*

Think about what is going on here. Peter has made this very emphatic statement that he would never deny or disown Jesus. I'm sure he was sincere when he said it and couldn't imagine himself in a position when he would ever deny knowing Jesus. All the other disciples said the same thing. Can't you picture them standing around shaking their heads saying, "Yea, me too, I will never deny you."

How do you think Peter felt when Jesus told him straight out that he would not be able to keep that vow he had just made, that he was going to fail. How would you feel if your best friend told you that when push came to shove you were going to bail?

How do you think Jesus must have felt as he looked at Peter, one of his best friends and told him, "You are going to fail me"? Don't you think He felt sorrow as well as betrayal? I mean He was human and He had to have felt something. I bet along with the pain of the betrayal, He felt sorrow for Peter, and what He knew Peter would have to go through.

Now let's skip down a few verses and reacquaint ourselves with what happened.

> *Now Peter was sitting out in the courtyard, and a servant girl came to him. "You also were with Jesus of Galilee," she said. But he denied it before them all. "I don't know what you're talking about," he said. Then he went out to the gateway, where another girl saw him and said to the people there, "This fellow was with Jesus of Nazareth."*
>
> *He denied it again, with an oath: "I don't know the man!" After a little while, those standing there went up to Peter and said, "Surely you are one of them, for your accent gives you away." Then he began to call down curses on himself and he swore to them, "I don't know the man!" Immediately a rooster crowed. Then Peter remembered the word Jesus had spoken: "Before the rooster crows, you will disown me three times." And he went outside and wept bitterly (Matthew 26:69-75).*

When did Peter realize what was happening? When the rooster crowed. This was like a trigger point for him because at that point he remembered what the Lord had said. Imagine what he must have been feeling. Big time failure and probably shame as he remembered himself standing in front of Jesus and all those other disciples loudly proclaiming: "even if.. I will never." What utter despair, shame and rejection he must have felt! They are all going to reject me and Jesus is going to reject me, I am a failure, I'm just a stupid fisherman, what made me think I could be anything else! Can't you just hear this going on in Peter's head?

Can you relate to Peter? When, if ever, have you felt like you betrayed Jesus? Maybe "betrayal" is too strong a word. How about "failed"? Ever felt that? Yea we have all dealt with failure. But Jesus is in the business of redemption. When you think about it isn't it interesting that both Judas and Peter caved in under pressure but they both reacted differently. Judas hung himself and Peter went back to being a fisherman. Judas must have felt he was beyond redemption, there was no hope. He had failed and betrayed Jesus and could never be forgiven. Peter probably felt that way but he just went back to doing what he did before he came in contact with Jesus. That's how he made his living, that's where he was comfortable.

Now this is where we get to the good part. This is where Peter moves beyond failure. This is where Jesus brings Peter back into restoration. In John 21 we find the disciples back on the Sea of Galilee fishing, just as they were when they first met Jesus. The disciples had struggled all night but caught nothing. And now they were tired, hungry and frustrated. Early in the morning Jesus showed up and He has built a fire and prepared breakfast for them on the beach. They are sitting around the fire and Peter is sitting there knowing he has miserably failed Jesus and in the eyes of the other disciples he probably feels a bit ashamed, probably trying to avoid eye contact with Jesus, making small talk like: "Hey, what have you been doing since you came back from the dead, just kind of hanging around walking through walls, that kind of stuff. Pretty cool. Me? Oh nothing much just mostly fishing, cleaning nets, the normal stuff."

When you have failed somebody or let them down how do you feel later when you see them? Isn't it hard to make eye contact with them? Don't you feel a bit embarrassed? Here he is again with Jesus, knowing Jesus knows what he did. As we read this story we realize that Jesus and Peter have come apart from the group and are walking alone down the beach. I can imagine Peter is expecting the worst. He's probably thinking, "Jesus is going to really tell me how He feels. I'll probably be told not to come around any more because I can't be trusted. Or He's going to tell me how much I've let Him down and how disappointed He is in me and what my failure has done to our friendship and how things will never be like they were before."

> *When they had finished eating, Jesus said to Simon Peter, "Simon son of John, do you truly love me more than these?" "Yes, Lord," he said, "you know that I love you."*
>
> *Jesus said, "Feed my lambs." Again Jesus said, "Simon son of John, do you truly love me?" He answered, "Yes, Lord, you know that I love you." Jesus said, "Take care of my sheep." The third time he said to him, "Simon son of John, do you love me?"*
>
> *Peter was hurt because Jesus asked him the third time, "Do you love me?" He said, "Lord, you know all things; you know that I love you." Jesus said, "Feed my sheep" (John 21:15-17).*

Many sermons have been preached about this, to try to learn why Jesus asked Peter this probing question three times. After the first time Peter answered, "Yes, Lord you know I love you." But he must have been in deep despair, thinking, "I may look bold on the outside but inside I'm a jellyfish. I actually denied and cursed the God of glory. I can't go back to being a fisher of men for Jesus' kingdom. I'm not worthy." Jesus interrupted his thoughts by repeating the question: "Peter, do you love me?" He was saying, in other words: Peter, this is what God really wants from you. It's not about your wisdom, your willpower or your works. All he wants is for you to love him more than anything in the world! Peter answered, "Lord, you know I love you."

But he still must have been thinking, "There's too much to understand. All these doctrines are too deep, too difficult to grasp. Others may get them, but they're beyond me. Sure, I have zeal, but it's without knowledge. I'm just an uneducated fisherman. I don't even understand the leading of the Lord. How could I ever live wholly dependent on him?" Finally, Jesus asked the disciple a third time: "Peter, do you love me?" And I believe this time, Peter got the message. Suddenly he says that knowing the Father was about more than reconciliation and rulership. It was also about having a relationship with Him!

This was a time of Jesus making it clear to Peter that he was forgiven, and still loved and valued by the Lord. In declaring his love for Jesus, Peter is restored as a committed believer and best of all; Jesus isn't finished with him yet. He still has plans and purposes for Peter's life. He has a new role for him. When He commissioned him before, it was as a fisher of men, but now he is to be one of the shepherds over the flock, the church in Jerusalem. Think about this: Would you have nominated Peter to be a leader in the Church? (Maybe, but he would be on probation).

Jack Hayford points out in his book *The Power and the Blessing*[1] that there was a reason why Peter's failure didn't destroy him. Before predicting that Peter would deny Him Jesus had said this:

> *Simon, Simon, Satan has asked to sift you as wheat.* ***But I have prayed for you Simon****, that your faith may not fail. And when you have turned back, strengthen your brothers"* *(Luke 22:31).*

There are two scriptures that should cause every believer to shout for joy.

> *Who is he that condemns? Christ Jesus, who died, more than that, who was raised to life, is at the right hand of God and is also interceding for us. (Romans 8:34)*

> *Therefore he is able to save completely those who come to God through him, because he always lives to intercede for them (Hebrews 7:25).*

Let me ask you this: Is there anything you have done or not done that has caused separation between you and God? Do you feel ashamed or embarrassed? Has your failure caused you also to feel rejection, to feel that God cannot or will not use you again? Let me assure you that regardless of past failures you are not beyond restoration. Come to Him and let Him restore you back into that relationship that He wants with you.

GOD'S LOVE IS BASED ON NOTHING

Perhaps you have heard someone say, "God loves you as you are and not as you should be!" I know we can easily accept this in our head without accepting it in our heart. We are so aware of our humanness that we find it difficult if not impossible to believe that God loves us unreservedly. We might even say His love is unreasonable.

We are so aware of our flaws, sins and frailties that it is difficult for us to come running and dancing into the presence of our Father who loves us as we are, where we are. We are comfortable with the idea of earning love by our works, or forgiveness by penance and passion, but not at ease with a love that is based on nothing we do, say, think, feel or imagine.

This whole idea of the unearned love of God can be very disturbing. Why struggle to do good? Won't the awareness that God loves us no matter what lead to spiritual laziness and moral looseness? I mean if God is going to love me anyway, why try so hard to earn it? Why be a good guy, attend church, tithe, volunteer to pass out food to the homeless? Why not go have some fun? Party on dude, eat, drink and be merry, for tomorrow we die. These appear to be sensible, valid questions.

In reality, quite the opposite is true. For example, I know that my wife loves me as I am and not as I should be. This is not an invitation to infidelity, indifference and an "anything goes" attitude. Quite the opposite. I travel a fair amount and often find myself in other states and countries far from home. This means I could do any number of things I wanted and no one would ever know, except me (and God). But my love for Jane keeps me from doing those things that would hurt her if she were to find out about them. Further, my love for others that would be devastated by my moral laxity. Just as my love for Jane keeps me from doing anything that would hurt her, my love for God keeps me from doing anything that would hurt Him. Jane's love calls forth love in me as God's love calls forth love in me. The more rooted we are in the love of God, the more generously we love our faith and practice it.

It is that kind of love that allows us to love ourselves without excuses and without questioning. We love ourselves as we are because we have been convinced that God does so. Some would say that loving ourselves is a form of pride. I believe that loving ourselves is a grateful dependence on God and a realistic appraisal of both our strengths and weaknesses.

When we discover that we are compatible and comfortable with a wide spectrum of people we will have come to terms with our own belovedness and humanness and will understand that Jesus sees us as flawed but good, wounded healers, children of the Father. We can then begin to pray as Thomas Merton did, "I thank God that I am like the rest of men."

We are special, created in His image, children of the Father, and we are human. We have flaws, warts, wrinkles and we sin. But we must understand we are loved and that His love is based on nothing that we do or don't do. Were it based on anything we do and that anything were to collapse, then God's love would crumble as well. That's not going to happen!

WHAT ABOUT THE INHERITANCE?

Thus far I have been addressing the lifestyle of one who is childlike but what I want to look at now is the inheritance of those who come to Jesus as little children. Oh yes, there is indeed an inheritance, which comes about as a result of our adoption, which is totally by his grace. *He predestined us to be adopted as his sons(children) through Jesus Christ, in accordance with his pleasure and will to the praise of his glorious grace, which he has freely given us in the One he loves* (Ephesians 1:5-6).

To be predestined means that God has determined beforehand that those who believe in Christ will be adopted into His family and conformed to His Son. But it does not relieve man of his responsibility to believe the gospel in order to bring to pass personally God's predestination and make it a reality. You may know firsthand what adoption means. Ideally when you were adopted you received all the same benefits and standing as would a natural child of the family that adopted you. Even if, like myself, you may not know firsthand what adoption means, we certainly know what privileges we had as a natural born child in a family.

We read further in Romans, *For you did not receive a spirit that makes you a slave again to fear, but you received the spirit of sonship. And by him we cry, "Abba, Father." The Spirit himself testifies with our spirit that we are God's children. Now if we are children, then we are heirs - heirs of God and co-heirs with Christ, if indeed we share in his sufferings in order that we may also share in his glory* (Romans 8:15-17). So we have all the privileges of Christ.

The first and foremost thing that comes to my mind is the love of God that he has lavished on us. *How great is the love the Father has lavished on us that we should be called children of God* (1 John 3:1). To lavish means to bestow in profusion; to give superabundantly, unrestrainedly, and generously.

Do you get the sense that this is good stuff?! Let's carry this a little further. In Matthew 28:18 Jesus says *"All authority in heaven and on earth has been given to me"*. Then in Luke when Jesus called the twelve disciples together it says he gave them power and authority to drive out all demons and to cure diseases, and he sent them out to preach the kingdom of God and to heal the sick. *"When Jesus had called the Twelve together, he gave them power and authority to drive out all demons and to cure diseases, and he sent them out to preach the kingdom of God and to heal the sick." Luke 9:1-2* Do we have this same authority and power? Yes! WHY? Because we are co-heirs with Christ!

Let me recap this for you.

First He says if you are even going to come into the kingdom of heaven you must turn from sin and consider your status or self-importance as insignificant. Entrance is by His grace not your works. Second, He says the kingdom of God belongs to those who are trusting, dependant, expectant. Lastly, not only will He lavish his love upon you but also He has given you power and authority to drive out demons, to cure diseases, and to heal the sick!

"LET'S REGAIN AND RETAIN THOSE CHILDLIKE QUALITIES THAT TRULY ALLOW GOD TO BOLDLY CLAIM US AS HIS CHILDREN AND HIS FRIENDS!"[2]

CONCLUSION

As I stated at the beginning of this book, from the moment of our birth until our death we deal with baggage that is the result of things that people say and do to us, as well as things we say and do to others and ourselves. For much of my life as a faithful believer these types of issues were never discussed. Therefore, I didn't have a clue that they existed and needed to be dealt with. Nor was any thought given to the fact that God would want me to deal with this baggage before I went home to be with Him.

Fortunately, over the course of many years of ministry, God taught me through personal experience, the writings of others and training at numerous conferences and workshops that this baggage not only exists but must be dealt with. What God clearly revealed to me was that He prefers we deal with it before we arrive to spend eternity with Him. He wants us to live an abundant, full and meaningful life NOW, before we get to heaven (John 10:10). That life doesn't happen if we live under the burden of the kind of baggage I have described in these chapters.

Admittedly I don't know what happens in heaven if we don't deal with baggage ahead of time. But what I do know is that Scripture clearly tells us that we are required to forgive as God has forgiven us. This is clear from the parable of the unforgiving servant in Matthew 18:21-35. It also says in Scripture that when we stand before God we will give an account of ourselves. *So then each of us will give an account of himself to God (Romans 14:12). Nothing in all creation is hidden from God's sight. Everything is uncovered and laid bare before the eyes of him to whom we must give account. (Hebrews 4:13).*

Wouldn't it be great to stand before him and say, "Father God, thank you for all the times you showed me the things deep in my heart of hearts that you were ready and willing to lift from my shoulders if I was willing to face and deal with them in your presence. What a journey toward wholeness you have led me through! I praise you with all my heart!"

I know from personal experience the significant changes I've seen in the lives of people as they have dealt with these issues. Mourning and depression have been replaced by joy and expectant hope, anger and bitterness removed and lives radically changed. I've watched as with tears streaming down their face their countenance changed from confusion and anger to understanding, freedom and joy.

If it was important enough for God to give me the title of this book, (remember the story I told in the preface) and help me write it, then it, is obviously something not to be taken lightly.

Now that you have read this book, the responsibility of what you are going to do with what you now know lies in your hands. If through the reading of this book God has revealed to you baggage that needs to be dealt with I strongly urge you to do that.

If you find you need help in doing this and you do not have someone that can be of assistance, contact our office in California and we will endeavor through Wholeness Ministries to either help you or put you in contact with someone that can help you.

Do not be discouraged but rather joyful that God loves you enough to want you to enjoy healing and wholeness right here, right now!

NOTES

Chapter 1 – The Traps of Unforgiveness
1. Ann Landers, Source Unknown
2. David Seamands, *Healing for Damaged Emotions* (N.P. Victor Books, 1992), p. 132.
3. Neil Anderson *Freedom in Christ Conference Handbook,* (January 24-27, 1995), p. 106.

Chapter 2 – A Look In The Mirror
1. Charles H. Kraft, *Deep Wounds, Deep Healing* (Ann Arbor, MI, Servant Publications, 1993)
2. David Seamands, *Healing for Damaged Emotions* (N.P. Victor Books, 1992), p. 99.
3. Source Unknown
4. Kraft, *p.169*
5. George S. Patton, Source Unknown
6. John Maxwell *Developing The Leader Within You* (Thomas Nelson, 2005), pp.145-146.

Chapter 3- I Will Never
1. *Merriam Webster's Collegiate Dictionary* (Tenth Edition, 1993)
2. John and Paula Sanford, *The Transformation of The Inner Man* (Tulsa, Victory House Inc. ,1982), p. 192.
3. Charles H. Kraft, *I Give You Authority,* (Chosen Books 1997), p.165
4. Source Unknown
5. Sanford, pp. 237-266 Summation of a teaching in their book.

6. Sanford, pp. 237-266 Summation of a teaching in their book.
7. Sanford, pp. 191-192
8. Kraft, pp. 165
9. Kraft, p. 166

Chapter 4 - Harmful Words, Harmful Connections
1. Charles H. Kraft, *I Give You Authority* (Grand Rapids, Chosen Books, 1997,) pp. 230-231 Summation of Kraft's teaching.
2. Kraft, p. 233.
3. Kraft, p. 233
4. Kraft, p. 233
5. Francis MacNutt, *Deliverance From Evil Spirits* (Grand Rapids, Chosen Books, 1995), p.129.
6. John and Paula Sanford, pp. 277-278.
7. Kraft, *pp.* 221-238 Summation of Kraft's teaching.

Chapter 5 - Let Yourself Be Loved By God
1. A. W. Tozer, *The Divine Conquest*, (New Jersey, Spire Books, 1950) Unable to locate page number.
2. Henry Nouwen, *Show Me The Way: Daily Lenten Readings* (The Crossroad Publishing Company, 1992), pp. 76-77.
3. Source Unknown
4. J.I. Packer, *Knowing God* (Intervarsity Press, 20th anniversary edition (June 24, 1993), Unable to locate page number.
5. Brennan Manning, *The Ragamuffin Gospel,* (Sisters, Oregon: Multnomah Publishers Inc. 1990), p. 149.
6. A.W. Tozer, *Man, The Dwelling Place of God*, (Harrisburg, PA: Christian Publications, 1966), pp. 9-10.
7. Author Unknown

Chapter 6 - The Recovery of Intimacy
1. Francis Frangipane, *Holiness, Truth and The Presence of God* (Advancing Church Publications, 1986), p. 13.
2. Dutch Sheets, *Intercessory Prayer (*Regal Books, 1996), p. 17.
3. Brennan Manning, *Abba's Child (*NavPress, 1994) p. 18.
4. Manning, p.48
5. Manning, p. 56.
6. Attributed to C. Raymond Beran, *Bits and Pieces*, 1992

Endnotes

Chapter 7 - God's Highest Purpose
1. Francis Frangipane, *The Three Battlegrounds* (Advancing Church Publications, 1989), pp. 34-38.
2. Brother Lawrence, *The Brother Lawrence Collection: Practice and Presence of God, Spiritual Maxims, the Life of Brother Lawrence* (Wilder Publications, 2008)), p. 51.
3. Andrew Murray, *Absolute Surrender* (Barbour Publishing, 2008), Unable to locate page number.
4. John Eldridge, *Wild At Heart: Discovering the Secret of a Man's Soul* (Thomas Nelson Books, 2001), p. 143.
5. Francis Frangipane, *The Three Battlegrounds*, p. 8

Chapter 8 - What God Will Not Accept
1. Francis Frangipane, *The Three Battlegrounds* (Advancing Church Publications, 1989), p. 65.
2. Francis Frangipane, "Beware - It is Easy to Fake Christianity"; from The Converging Zone website, at: http://www.convergingzone.com/ricciardelli/beware-it-is-easy-to-fake-christianity-by-francis-frangipane
3. Thomas Merton, *New Seeds of Contemplation* (New Directions Publishing Corporation, 1961), p. 174.
4. Richard Foster, *Prayer* (San Francisco, Harper, 1992), p.1
5. Brennan Manning, *Abba's Child*, p.31
6. A. W. Tozer, *The Divine Conquest* (Old Tappan: Spire Books, 1950), p. 25.
7. Henry Nouwen/Richard Foster, *Leadership*, Christianity Today, 1984

Chapter 9 - Unless You Change And Become As Little Children
1. Jack W. Hayford, *The Power and the Blessing* (N.P. Victor Books, 1994), p.48
2. I believe this was said by Francis Frangipane, but I have been unable to locate the original source.

ABOUT MIKE EVANS

Mike Evans is the Founder and Director of Wholeness Ministries located in Bakersfield, CA. Mike is a graduate of Golden Gate University and earned his Masters Degree in Christian Education at Mennonite Brethren Biblical Seminary and was ordained in 1982. Mike was an associate pastor from 1976 to 1994 at Bakersfield Christian Life Center. In 1989 Mike founded Wholeness Ministries. Our purpose and mission is to continue Jesus' work by praying for healing and training and equipping believers to effectively minister to those in need of healing, in the physical, emotional and spiritual areas of their lives. Using his book *Learning To Do What Jesus Did,* Mike and his team have ministered healing in Kuwait, Qatar, N.Ireland, England, Puerto Rico, Hungary, Romania, India, Korea and extensively throughout the United States.

Jesus not only proclaimed the Gospel, but he demonstrated the power of God through miracles and by healing the sick and freeing those oppressed by the evil one. "Mike says, based on my understanding of Luke 4:18-19, I believe that God is calling us as never before to do the works of His Kingdom: to release the oppressed, heal the sick and proclaim the Good News. It is my desire to bring the Christian's permission and authority to heal back into the mainstream of all denominations of the church."

Why Not Waste Time With God? "Along with healing prayer, I am equally passionate about moving beyond a superficial relationship with God to live in intimacy with Him. Churches are increasingly bringing me in to spend entire weekends teaching on spiritual renewal and intimacy using my book *Why Not Waste Time With God.*"

"I am also committed to reaching young adults with this epic message of healing and moving beyond a superficial relationship with God to a place of genuine intimacy with Him."

ABOUT WHOLENESS MINISTRIES

The Church has a mission. In fact it has a mandate to carry on Jesus' original mission: to bind up the broken-hearted, to heal the sick, to set free those in bondage. Learning to be like Jesus – continuing His mission – doing the same things that He did – that is the Christian life at its most simple.

EQUIPPED FOR MINISTRY

For the past twenty years, Mike Evans the founder of Wholeness Ministries has been known for being passionate about one thing above all other things: teaching followers of Jesus how to make healing prayer a normal part of their daily life. To know how to pray for the sick at the grocery store, the mall, where we pick up our morning coffee, etc. Through his book, Learning To Do What Jesus Did, you will learn that this can become normal for all believers.

PRAYER TEAM TRAINING

Many churches and ministries have utilized Mike's passion in helping them develop a well-grounded and well-trained team of prayer ministers who are soundly equipped to handle the physical, spiritual, and emotional needs of others. Mike offers a wide range of materials for those looking to expand their prayer ministries in their church, or to find learning materials to study personally.

PERSONAL MINISTRY

Do you or someone you know need prayer for physical, emotional, or spiritual healing? The deep healing of our brokenness, whether it's physical, emotional, or spiritual, is often something we are incapable of accomplishing on our own. Through intensive, incisive prayer sessions, Mike has been able to help numerous people discover levels of freedom and release from emotional and spiritual bondage that they never imagined possible.

HEALING CONFERENCES

Wholeness Ministries' founder Mike Evans is a highly sought-after speaker and lecturer on many specific topics relating to healing, and praying effectively. Wholeness Ministries can specifically structure seminars around a wide variety of different issues, including dealing with the traps of unforgiveness, healing the Wounded Self-Image, healing the Father wound, and identifying Inner Vows and how to renounce them.

HEALING SERVICES

Are you looking for somebody to lead a "healing service" in your church, or even a "healing crusade" in your city? We'd love to be a part of your vision! Wholeness Ministries is geared to be a part of your special Healing Event. All you need to do is provide the venue and get the word out to your community – we'll do the rest!

FREEDOM SEMINAR

FREEDOM! Seminar and Retreat is designed to address a wide variety of issues, using Mike's latest book, Before You Get Here. Subtitled, "Baggage To Drop On Your Way To Heaven," it is a guide to assist in discovering freedom from the invisible burdens that oppress and defeat many Christians today. Topics included are: The Traps of Unforgiveness, Healing the Wounded Self-Image, Healing the Father Wound, Breaking Curses and Soul Ties and Understanding Inner Vows and how to renounce them.

The FREEDOM! Seminar can be set up to accommodate what would work best in your setting. Typically, they are done locally here in Bakersfield, CA. We meet once a week for four weeks and end with an all day Saturday retreat session when our trained prayer teams minister to the participants. The seminar can also be structured to be conducted on a Thursday night, all day Friday and Saturday. We are flexible and willing to work with what works best for you.

Wholeness Ministries is looking forward to providing your church with a tailor-made weekend to meet your needs! Do you want to talk to someone about booking a conference or retreat with Wholeness Ministries at your church? Whether it's next month or next year that you are looking to schedule give us a call!

To schedule a Wholeness Ministries training conference, or to receive additional information, please contact:

Wholeness Ministries
P.O. Box 80503
Bakersfield, CA 93380 U.S. A.
Phone: 661-833-2920
E-Mail: mevans@wholeness.org
www.wholeness.org

www.ingramcontent.com/pod-product-compliance
Lightning Source LLC
Chambersburg PA
CBHW031423290426
44110CB00011B/500